W9-AOV-951

Ethnicity and Suburban Local Politics

David J. Schnall

The Praeger Special Studies program—utilizing the most modern and efficient book production techniques and a selective worldwide distribution network—makes available to the academic, government, and business communities significant, timely research in U.S. and international economic, social, and political development.

Ethnicity and Suburban Local Politics

PRAEGER SPECIAL STUDIES IN U.S. ECONOMIC, SOCIAL, AND POLITICAL ISSUES

Praeger Publishers   New York   Washington   London

Library of Congress Cataloging in Publication Data

Schnall, David J
  Ethnicity and suburban local politics.

  (Praeger special studies in U.S. economic, social,
and political issues)
  Bibliography: p.
  Includes index.
  1. Local government—United States. 2. Ethnic
attitude. 3. Suburbs—United States. I. Title.
JS341.S33   1975   324'.2   74-19825
ISBN 0-275-05820-4

PRAEGER PUBLISHERS
111 Fourth Avenue, New York, N.Y. 10003, U.S.A.

Published in the United States of America in 1975
by Praeger Publishers, Inc.

Printed in the United States of America

To my beloved wife Tova whose love, loyalty, and devotion serve as inspiration for all my endeavors

To my dear parents, Mr. and Mrs. Harry Schnall, for their encouragement and loving guidance

To the blessed memories of Yehoshua Roth and Avigdor Schnall for the legacy of perseverance and goodwill they left to me

Much effort has been expended over the past twenty-
five years in attempting to understand the factors which
go into the choices and general political attitudes of
the American electorate. Many leading scholars have indicated that certain variables, including issues, party affiliation, candidate preference, and socioeconomic status,
are important influences upon the vote. In certain instances one or another factor has been given greater
weight, while at other times various combinations of factors have been utilized. However, despite these important studies, significant lapses exist in the level and
scope of the data, and it is generally recognized that no
adequate systematic theories have been devised to explain
the various manifestations of voting behavior and political attitudes.

To illustrate these gaps, it is most noticeable that,
while much emphasis has been placed upon the study of national elections--using data gathered nationally or in one
locality--little has been done to analyze and explain
voter activity at the local level. Similarly, even those
studies of various localities have concentrated upon the
political responses and activities of those localities in
national elections. By and large, the issue of how these
same voters respond in elections of a purely local nature,
as well as their attitudes about these elections and the
politics they represent, is an area that has been ignored.

As a result, a number of interesting questions remain
yet to be answered. These questions are essential to the
development of a systematic theory of political participation. In the first instance, while several political and
demographic variables have been found to relate significantly to voter choice and attitudes at the national level,
it is unclear whether these same variables would remain
significant in politics of a purely local nature. If, indeed, these variables lose some of their significance at
the local level, what other variables might replace them?

Such a set of possibilities lend themselves to important inferences. Is it perhaps possible that certain
variables--either because of their very nature or the nature of local politics--cannot be significant in the political arena? If so, then the isolation of these factors
and the study of their interplay (or its lack) at the local

level may prove invaluable to the general understanding of electoral politics.

These questions take on more than academic importance if the local arena under discussion happens to be suburban. In the past twenty-five years, a massive exodus of central-city dwellers to the adjacent suburbs has been witnessed. As more suburbs attract more residents, more voters are eligible to participate in the local suburban political arena. Which variables are important to the suburban voter in local elections, and which are unimportant to him, are obviously vital issues. Understanding his responses also presupposes an understanding of his attitudes, interests, and propensities to participate. Intensive research is needed to study voter choice, participation, and interest in purely local politics, and the attitudes of suburban voters in the local political arena.

Parallel to the issue of suburban local politics lies the question of the importance of religion, race, and nationality in such an electoral setting. Comprehensively referred to as ethnicity, this variable has been assigned diverse importance by various leading scholars. In one form or another, several analysts have commented on the role of ethnicity in politics. Generally, conclusions have ranged from the inevitable demise of ethnicity as a factor in local politics to its influence as an idiosyncratic element in the politics of particular sections of northeastern cities (notably Boston, New York, and New Haven) in which still reside elderly immigrants or their children.

Little effort has been made, however, to study the influence of the ethnic variable on local suburban politics. As the authors of a recent study of ethnic voting on the national level concluded: "Survey analysis of the non-ghettoized ethnics, a costly proposition to be sure, must be undertaken if a complete political profile is to be drawn."[1]

Such survey analysis would suggest answers to many questions raised by the present discussion. A clearer understanding of the role of ethnicity in electoral politics might be expected to emerge. Thus, is ethnicity a passing or idiosyncratic political variable or does it maintain its importance even outside certain urban communities? Perhaps what has been generally assumed about the minimal or declining role of ethnicity in politics is true only in relation to national politics. Elections of "lower visibility" may manifest continued and strengthened ethnic influence.

Further, if it should be found that ethnicity is a
significant suburban variable, will this significance manifest itself in terms of race, religion, nationality, or
some combination of these ethnic components? Equally,
might it be expected that fellow-ethnics (those of the
same ethnic group) will vote alike for fellow-ethnic candidates . . . or both? Finally, how will ethnicity compare with other political variables such as class status,
party affiliation, issue orientation, and political interest in the voting, attitudes, and interest levels of suburban residents.

The present study, therefore, is intended to help
fill the gap in the existing literature relative to the
suburban political arena generally and the importance of
ethnicity within it specifically. It should be noted
that ethnicity as a political variable has taken on re-
newed importance to journalists in light of the recent
political awakenings of various nonwhite and Hispanic-
American communities, as well as the political strategies
of national and local political leaders among "white ethnics." The present study may also add to the academic
understanding of these events and suggest inferential
directions.

In sum, the ensuing analysis hopes to suggest answers
to the questions raised above. It will attempt to determine the influence of variables studied in national elections upon the attitudes, interests, and voting habits of
suburban residents in purely local elections, and the
salience of ethnicity in these political attitudes, interests, and choices.

NOTE

1. M. Kramer and M. Levey, The Ethnic Factor (New
York: Simon & Schuster, 1972), pp. 223-24.

A deep and abiding fear is to be found in the heart of most authors when they are about to enumerate their acknowledgments. It relates to the possibility that the name of some individual who was involved in the creation of the volume will be overlooked and neglected. This fear is particularly present when the work is one such as this and includes both substantive and technical analysis. I begin with an apology, therefore, to any worthy individuals whose names have been accidentally omitted.

In substantive terms, I am most especially indebted to my mentor, colleague, and close friend, Professor Stephen David of Fordham University, whose guidance and instruction is evident in each section of this work and whose influence upon my thinking has been profound. In addition, I wish to acknowledge the patient and sincere aid of Professor Martin Fergus and the incisive comments of Professor Richard Regan, S.J. The joint efforts of these three gentlemen served to shape and frame the context of the research and the thrust of its analysis.

I also wish to express my gratitude to Professors Joseph Ball and Paul Kantor who read earlier drafts of the manuscript. Their advice and suggestions were invaluable in adding form to the present volume.

In implementing the technical aspects of the research, I received considerable aid from my colleagues and supervisors at Staten Island Community College. Especially deserving of mention are Dean Leonard Kreisman, Mr. Eugene Stein, and the Internal Grants Committee, whose generosity and support allowed me to complete my research. In addition, the creative ability of Mr. Thomas Branniff and Ms. Janet Goldwasser of the Computer Center at Staten Island Community College facilitated my analysis of the data and allowed me considerable freedom in its compilation. Further, Ms. Flo Bergin's talents as a typist were fundamental to the completion of the original manuscript.

I am also deeply indebted to my supervisor and friend Dean Joseph Harris of the College Discovery Program. His confidence and encouragement serve as inspiration to all who work with him. I also wish to acknowledge the aid of my friends and colleagues at S.I.C.C., whose fellowship and good nature create a conducive atmosphere for accomplishment and creative scholarship.

I must finally indicate the inspiration and guidance of those individuals to whom this volume is dedicated. Their role in my personal development cannot be measured. May the publication of this work serve as a small tribute to their kindness and love. While the contributions of each of the above to the publication of this volume were considerable, I must claim full responsibility for any errors found herein.

CONTENTS

LIST OF TABLES AND FIGURES

Figure | Page

Ethnicity and
Suburban Local Politics

1

VOTING,
ETHNICITY, AND
SUBURBIA: AN OVERVIEW

The process by which Americans formulate their attitudes and decide whether or not to vote, and for whom, is
one that has intrigued scholars and journalists for many
years. The present effort is one among many studies to
attempt to determine the details of this delicate and
complex process within the suburban political arena, one
which has been sorely neglected or subject to erroneous
generalization in the past. Prior to the analysis of the
present data, it would be well, however, to review briefly
that which has been written about suburban voting in the
past and to discuss those areas to which the present data
may relate, as well as those gaps which it may help to fill.

VOTING IN THE SUBURBS

The two classic studies of voting behavior are The
People's Choice and Voting, the first a landmark study of
Erie County, Ohio, and the second a follow-up study of
Elmira, New York.[1] Each of these areas was chosen by the
authors as representative of the country as a whole, and
panel interviews were held to determine the motivations
and attitudes of the voters. Among other findings, the
data indicated that some two-thirds of the electorate
made decisions months before the election took place. It
should be noted that these works concentrated on the presidential elections of 1940 and 1948 respectively, so that
little was done to examine voter activity or attitudes
toward Erie County or Elmira per se.
The work of Angus Campbell and the Survey Research
Center at the University of Michigan stands in structural

and methodological contrast to these studies. Rather than use a single area as a model and administer intensive panel interviews there, Campbell drew a national sample of some 2,000 respondents and interviewed them once just before and once just after the presidential election.[2] Campbell concluded that political attitudes are the result of three variables: (1) the voter's party preference, (2) his issue orientation, and (3) his candidate preference. He further determined that some 11.5 percent of the electorate were able to present what could be realistically considered a personal political ideology, while the rest were less politically sophisticated. He concluded that there exists a "funnel of causality" which represents the voter's decision-making process and results in the vote. Nearest to the mouth of the funnel are the voter's politically salient "attitudes," which are based upon the three variables earlier mentioned. Still further back lie the psychosocial variables such as class, religion, and education. It was upon this base that much of the work done in the suburbs was attempted.

The first significant systematic theories dealing with suburban political participation were formulated in the mid-fifties. The most evident finding was that the suburbs were overwhelmingly Republican, and the progressive exodus to the suburbs was resulting in apparently substantial increases in Republican strength there. The problem of explaining the effect of the move to the suburbs upon the previously Democratic city dweller was attacked from two levels. Key argued that new suburbanites, for reasons of both value-orientation and self-interest, were ready converts to the suburban creed of Republicanism. Lubell, however, claimed that the move to the suburbs was not the cause of the change but merely a manifestation of the more significant trend of upward mobility, of which increased Republicanism is another barometer. Thus the new suburbanites were not being converted, they were merely transplanting their values to their new communities.[3]

While each of the theories may have had considerable validity, they both were based upon an erroneous assumption: that moving to the suburbs means voting Republican. This assumption was tested in a number of follow-up studies and found to be inaccurate. Janosik, Wood, and Banfield and Wilson[4] all found the contrary to be the case; that is, in the areas of the greatest influx of central-city dwellers, either the Republican majority was substantially reduced or the area shifted from Republican to Democratic

entirely. Berger,[5] upon reaching a similar conclusion
offered the following tentative explanation. In fact,
suburban areas have no real political ethos. Rather, the
new resident simply continues his political development
with no change necessarily taking place in his political
identification.

The election of 1960 conclusively disproved the belief in monolithic suburban political identification and
encouraged the parallel development of studies which
tested the homogeneity of the suburbs on all scales.
Berger, Lazerwitz, and Wirt[6] concluded in turn that not
only were there working-class areas in various suburbs,
but indeed many suburbs were predominantly working class.
Further, of 154 suburbs studied by Wirt, only 52 percent
could be classified at least "modified one-party Republican" based on electoral data from 1932-60. It should be
noted that only national electoral data was used. One
might well wonder whether findings would be similar in
purely local elections, especially in nonpresidential
election years when national influences were not present.
Further, while Berger claims that no political ethos exists in the suburbs, and the voter simply continues his
political development, no effort has been made to separate
the national or state from the purely local. Thus it is
no secret that the smaller the arena, the lower the political competition level. This inheres in the fact that
larger electoral units include greater numbers of voters
who are therefore more likely to be diverse. While a congressional election or councilmanic race may include only
a small and limited electorate from a local community, a
senatorial election includes all the various and diverse
voters in a state. The possibilities for competition are
much greater at these larger levels where many different
types of voters may be attracted.[7] Indeed the South is a
perfect example of this theory--increased party competition
in national elections with little change at the local
scene. It may be that what Berger defines as a "lack of
political ethos" is in fact a lack of national political
ethos. Toward local affairs this ethos may be well developed. If it is, then, in such purely local elections,
what are the factors that are most important to the voter?

Similarly, since national elections generate the most
excitement and interest among voters, it is not unreasonable to assume that elections of a purely local nature
will result in lower levels of interest and may well re-
veal little interest in either local partisanship or local
politics in general. This, too, is an area that must be

studied independent of the influences of a national election.

In all of the above, the underlying assumption is that indeed there are differences between the factors involved in national or other "high-visibility" elections and local ones. This assumption in itself indicates the need for intensive study of purely local politics. Lacking such data, the following analysis of the traditionally studied variables is tentatively presented.

While there is no question that the party label plays a large role in national elections, it may well be that party is not important to the suburban voter in local politics. The move to the suburbs may not transform or convert the voter, but it also does not leave him totally unaffected. Party loyalties felt in the city will not be felt as strongly, if at all, in the suburbs. It may not be surprising to find a high degree of partisan independence, while even those voters who identify with a party may not consider themselves "strong" Democrats or "strong" Republicans. This may be even truer of purely local elections in which the voter, even if he does have strong partisan tendencies nationally, may not perceive any difference between either party or their candidates on the local scene. It is precisely the "low visibility" of the local political arena that may make inferences from national data highly suspect. What Berger has termed "the lack of political ethos" may in effect be merely the lack of "visibility." It is precisely this crucial difference between the lack of ethos and the lack of visibility that may influence each of the factors which go into voting, attitudes, and interest in suburban local politics.

Much of the same may be true of issues. Local elections are "low visibility" elections which do not generate much interest. Real issues may exist in these elections but they may not be perceived by the voter, either because of a genuine lack of interest or because of a lack of exposure to local sources of information. Further, even if the voter does sense the existence of issues and the relevance of his own opinions to them, he may be prevented from voting along issue lines because he does not perceive there to be significant differences between candidates. For "issues" to be an important electoral factor, they must: (1) be recognizable to the voter as such, (2) appear relevant to his own attitudes, and (3) imply perceivable differences between candidates. It may be that some, if not all of these factors will be absent on the local scene. Further, even assuming that these factors

are present, they play no role if the voter is not aware
of them. Therefore, whether or not the voter is regularly
exposed to local channels of information will also affect
the importance of "issues." It may be that the voter pays
little attention to these "issues" even when they do exist.

Another much studied variable is social class. This
has been determined either by annual income, occupation,
education, value of dwelling, or some combination thereof.
Class may influence the vote in one of three ways. Either
the voter will: (1) perceive that a particular candidate
better represents his financial needs and socioeconomic
interests, or (2) choose a particular candidate because he
has a similar socioeconomic status to the voter's own, or
(3) remain loyal to a particular party because he believes
that party best represents the interests of the voter's
class. Yet each of these aspects of socioeconomic status
as a political variable carries inherent difficulties.
In order for the voter to perceive that a given candidate
better represents his financial and socioeconomic needs,
all that has been said in regard to "issues" must once
again be true. In addition, the voter must be sophisticated enough to understand his own self-interests, the
implications of policy proposals, and the connections
between these and the individual candidates. This does
not seem likely.

Similarly, in order for the voter to choose a candidate because his socioeconomic status is similar to the
voter's own, the voter must be aware of the candidate's
social class and have a choice between candidates of
various social classes. This too is unlikely because the
social class of a candidate is not apparent from the
ballot, and most local candidates are typically middle-
class professionals.

While loyalty to a particular political party based
upon the belief that the party best represents the socioeconomic values of the given voter remains as a possibility, much the same can be said of it as has been said of
local partisanship and would be detected in tests of local partisanship in any case.

ETHNICITY AND THE SUBURBS

In lieu of the above variables, and in search of an
element which may simplify his choice, the suburban voter
will turn to ethnicity, as it is recognizable from the
candidate's name. This need results from the confusion

5

the suburban voter may feel because of the irrelevance of
the other variables as previously discussed. Thus it may
be expected that voters of similar ethnic affiliation
(racial, religious, and national in that order) will tend
to vote for candidates of the same group. This they will
tend to do more often than depend upon other factors mentioned.

In addition, a second impact of ethnicity upon local
politics may also be delineated, aside from the ethnic
identification of the candidate, which may serve as a cue
to the voter of that same group. The identity of the
voter may influence the vote independently from that of
the candidate. It may be that because of many similar
experiences and interactions, voters of similar ethnic
identity will vote and think alike. This may result from
similar perceptions of issues, similar value systems, or
similar needs. It may therefore be hypothesized that
voters of the same ethnic identity will tend to vote alike
--whether for "ethnic candidates" or for others--and will
also tend to have similar attitudes and interest levels.
As with the first influence of ethnicity outlined above,
this second form of influence will surface more often
than will relationships based upon other variables.

It should be noted that the concept of a lingering
ethnic identification with implications for political
choice has not generally been accorded scholarly accep-
tance. Perhaps many authors agree with Robert Dahl that
the strength of ethnic ties ". . . as a factor in local
politics must surely recede."[8] Nevertheless, sociological
data exists to the contrary. Lenski, Kramer and Levantman,
and Carlos,[9] all found attendance at religious services
and participation in religious-communal life to be on the
increase among second- and third-generation Americans.
For the present purposes it is significant that both
Lenski and Carlos did considerable work in the suburbs.
They both concluded that religious affiliation in the
suburbs served more a social than spiritual function in
fulfilling the values of community identity and integration.

Equally, Lieberson,[10] in a study of ethnic segregation in residential patterns found there to be an equal
degree of ethnic residential segregation when comparing
city dwellers with suburban residents, for the period
1930-50. Apparently, ethnic preferences and identities
extend themselves, in some form, to the suburbs. Indeed,
Parenti has argued that, aside from his occupation, it is
not unlikely that the suburbanite exists within an ethnic

community that serves most all his social needs.[11] It is therefore not unreasonable to assume that the ethnic affiliation of an individual will affect his political perceptions. In addition, it may be noted that Wolfinger has argued that the strength of the ethnic group in the political realm does not truly surface until the third or fourth generation, often the one which leaves the city for the suburbs.[12]

In more specifically political terms, it is relevant to note the work of Banfield and Wilson in Cayuga County, Hawkins and Lorinskas in Chicago, Pomper in Newark, and Kramer and Levey nationally.[13] Banfield and Wilson studied the role of ethnicity in the articulation of politically relevant attitudes and refined the concepts of "immigrant" and "Yankee" political ethos in terms of "public-regarding" or "private-regarding" attitudes toward taxes and government expenditures. They found there to be discernible differences between Anglo-Saxon Protestants and East European Catholics, with Jews closer to the Protestants and Blacks generally close to the Catholics. Pomper, in a study of nonpartisan elections, found that when the comfort of the party label is removed, the voter tends to use the ethnic identity as a referent. Employing a "controlled ballot," Hawkins and Lorinskas compared central-city residents with suburban-rural residents of the same ethnic background (in this case Polish) and confirmed Pomper's findings in both localities. Finally, Kramer and Levey made a nationwide attempt to delineate the relative strength of ethnic identification among six major ethnic groups, using aggregate data from a sample of 2,000 precincts. Their data indicated there to be distinguishable electoral trends which differentiate these groups from each other.

Given the assumed weaknesses of many other sociopolitical and demographic variables within the suburban political sphere, as well as the findings of those other analysts who have studied ethnicity in relation to politics, this research enters with the supposition that ethnicity will prove to be of major significance in suburban electoral politics. This significance will manifest itself both in objective terms as well as comparative terms. The present study will therefore serve to test not only the simple significance of ethnicity in the suburbs but also its significance compared to, or combined with, such other factors as party affiliation, social class, issue orientations and attitudes, candidate perception, and political interest and participation.

It should be noted that the influence of ethnicity may be measured in two manners. It may be tested in terms of the degree to which voters of a given ethnic group tend to vote for fellow-members who happen to be candidates for election. In addition, it may be tested in terms of the degree to which voters of similar ethnic identification tend to vote similarly irrespective of the ethnic identity of the candidates. Both these manifestations will be tested.

Further, it is also valuable to recognize that the various manifestations of political/electoral activity may be divided and categorized. This will facilitate the study of ethnicity within each area and its comparison with diverse other variables. Therefore, ethnicity will be tested in relation to the stated electoral preferences of the voters, their attitudes in several major issue-areas, and their levels of political interest and partic-ipation. In each area, ethnicity will be tested as an independent political variable, and its influence will be statistically compared to that of other selected socio-political and demographic factors.

For the purposes of strict analysis and scientific precision, such a set of assumptions cannot be left in amorphous language, though it may truly reflect the induc-tive nature of the research. To satisfy the requirements of socioscientific inquiry, therefore, the following hy-potheses may serve to frame the research:

1. Ethnicity will be of greater importance than any other variable in voter choice for local suburban elec-tions.

- Ethnicity will be more important than party affiliation, social class, issue positions, interest levels, or candidate perception.
- Members of similar ethnic groups will have a greater tendency to vote for candidates whom they perceive to be of their own group (as recognizable from the candidate's last name) than any others, in local elections.
- Members of similar ethnic groups will tend to vote similarly irrespective of the ethnic identification of the candidate.

2. On tests of general policy orientation, there will be a greater relationship between political attitudes and ethnicity than between political attitudes and any other single variable.

- Voters of similar ethnic identification tend to view things similarly.

- Ethnicity will be more important than party affiliation, social class, issue interest, or candidate perception.

3. There will be a greater relationship between ethnicity and interest in local politics than between interest and any other political variable.

- Interest is defined in terms of nonvoting, the tendency to follow local politics on the local radio, in local newspapers, or to discuss it with friends and relatives, as well as the self-assessed interest levels of the voters.
- A stronger relationship will be found between ethnicity and interest in local politics than between interest and social class, party affiliation, attitude, or candidate perceptions.

With the concepts and variables now set in context, it is possible to proceed properly with the present study, indicating its significance in terms of the hypotheses presented and the work done in the field by other researchers.

NOTES

1. B. Berelson et al., The People's Choice (New York: Columbia University, 1948), and B. Berelson et al., Voting (Chicago: University of Chicago, 1954).

2. A. Campbell et al., The Voter Decides (New York: Harper & Bros., 1954), and A. Campbell et al., The American Voter (New York: John Wiley & Sons, 1960).

3. V. O. Key, American State Politics (New York: Knopf, 1956), and S. Lubell, The Future of American Politics (New York: Harper & Bros., 1952).

4. G. Janosik, "The New Suburbia," Current History (August 1956): 91-95; R. Wood, Suburbia: Its People and Their Politics (Boston: Houghton Mifflin Co., 1959), especially pp. 145-49; E. Banfield and J. Wilson, City Politics (Cambridge: Harvard University and M.I.T., 1963), p. 241.

5. B. Berger, Working-Class Suburb (Berkeley: University of California, 1960).

6. P. Lazerwitz, "Suburban Voting Trends: 1948 to 1956," Social Forces (October 1960): 29-36; F. Wirt, "The Political Sociology of American Suburbia: A Reinterpretation," Journal of Politics (August 1965): 647-66.

9

7. R. Dahl, <u>Pluralist Democracy in the United States</u> (Chicago: Rand McNally & Co., 1967), pp. 218-19.

8. R. Dahl, <u>Who Governs</u> (New Haven: Yale University, 1961), pp. 59-62.

9. G. Lenski, <u>The Religious Factor</u> (Garden City: Doubleday & Co., 1961); J. Kramer and S. Levantman, <u>Children of the Gilded Ghetto</u> (New Haven: Yale University, 1961); S. Carlos, "Religious Participation and the Urban-Suburban Continuum," <u>American Journal of Sociology</u> (March 1970): 742-59.

10. S. Lieberson, "Suburbs and Ethnic Residential Patterns," <u>American Journal of Sociology</u> (May 1962): 673-81.

11. M. Parenti, "Ethnic Politics and the Persistence of Ethnic Identification," <u>American Political Science Review</u> (December 1967): 717-26.

12. R. Wolfinger, "The Development and Persistence of Ethnic Voting," <u>American Political Science Review</u> (December 1965): 896-908.

13. E. Banfield and J. Wilson, "Public-Regardedness as a Value Premise in Voting Behavior," <u>American Political Science Review</u> (September 1965): 876-87. See also their "Political Ethos Revisited," <u>American Political Science Review</u> (December 1971): 1048-62; R. Lorinskas and B. Hawkins, "The Persistence of Ethnic Voting in Urban and Rural Areas," <u>Social Science Quarterly</u> (March 1969): 891-99; G. Pomper, "Ethnic and Group Voting in Non-Partisan Municipal Elections," <u>Public Opinion Quarterly</u> (Spring 1966): 79-97; M. Levey and M. Kramer, <u>The Ethnic Factor</u> (New York: Simon & Schuster, 1972).

2

THE PRESENT DATA

THE SETTING

Obviously, in a comprehensive analysis such as this, it is to be expected that unanticipated propositions and conclusions may emerge from the data. To test those specifically delineated above, an intensive survey of a random sampling of registered voters in the suburban town of Ramapo, New York, was drawn. The town is a subdivision of Rockland County, some 25 miles north of New York City. Rockland is the fourth largest nonurban county in New York State (after Suffolk, Nassau, and Westchester) and Ramapo is the largest of the townships in Rockland. Ramapo experienced a massive 118.7 percent population increase since 1960, which suggests the great exodus of central-city dwellers to this adjacent suburb in the past decade. The town's population is well distributed among village areas, which are incorporated and generally less affluent, and the more traditionally suburban unincorporated areas.

In general, Ramapo is not significantly different, in demographic terms at least, from other suburban communities in the New York City area. This can be easily demonstrated.

Table 2.1 presents a comparison of Ramapo with the other major New York suburban areas in economic terms. As the data indicate, all five areas are relatively affluent communities. Nevertheless, Ramapo is not particularly unusual among them. It ranks first in median income, second--behind Westchester--in median cost of house and second--behind Nassau--in terms of median contract rent. This implies that Ramapo, while housing a wealthy group of residents, is not uncharacteristically affluent by the standards of New York City metropolitan suburbia. This fact is also reflected in socioeconomic data relating to the areas of occupation and education. These data are presented in Table 2.2.

TABLE 2.1

Economic Comparison of Ramapo With
Other New York Suburbs

Locality	Median Income (in dollars)	Median Cost of House (in dollars)	Median Monthly Contract Rent (in dollars)
Ramapo	15,813	40,328	156
Rockland	13,100	34,200	142
Westchester	13,784	40,500	129
Nassau	14,632	30,200	159
Suffolk	12,084	24,100	146

Source: Rockland County Planning Board.

TABLE 2.2

Social Comparison of Ramapo With
Other New York Suburbs

Locality	Percent White Collar	Median School Years
Ramapo	64	12.7
Rockland	70	12.7
Westchester	64	13.2
Suffolk	58	12.6
Nassau	63	12.9

Source: Rockland County Planning Board.

As is evident from Table 2.2, the town of Ramapo is quite similar to Rockland generally and to the other suburban counties in the New York City area as well. Ramapo ranks second--along with Westchester and only one percentage point ahead of Nassau--in terms of percentage of the work force in white collar or professional occupations. Interestingly, Rockland as a whole ranks first in

this classification. In addition, Ramapo ranks third--
along with Rockland generally--in terms of median number
of school years completed. On both of these measures,
and indeed by all the various standards here employed,
all the suburban areas being compared are quite similar
and none appear to be unusual or atypical.

It would be erroneous to assume, however, that no
diversity exists. Politically, for example, 31.4 percent
of Ramapo's voters are registered Republicans, while 48.4
percent are registered Democrats. This did not prevent
Mr. Nixon from winning a decisive victory there in 1972,
nevertheless. In addition, some 6.5 percent of the population is nonwhite, largely Black, and lives in an area
known as the "hill" in the village of Spring Valley.
Curiously, the Ramapo delegation to the county legisla-
ture has been largely Republican, while the Democrats
held a majority on the 1972 town board. In addition, the
town supervisor is a Democrat.

Indeed, the very fact that the elections held in
Ramapo are partisan elections is an interesting characteristic. Many suburban and middle-size cities have chosen
to eliminate the use of the party label of candidates on
the ballot. An earlier noted study of Newark (see p. 7)
indicated that, under such circumstances, ethnicity tends
to replace party affiliation in simplifying the voter's
decision. Therefore, the fact that the Ramapo elections
are partisan may in fact enhance the study in terms of
the previously listed hypotheses. The setting for the
study is one in which the hypotheses have least chance of
confirmation, that is, if ethnicity operates to replace
party affiliation in its absence, it may not so operate
in its presence. Thus, if it should be found that ethnicity is of greatest importance to the suburban voter in
a town which holds partisan elections, it may be fairly
assumed that such would be the case in areas having non-
partisan elections. Conversely, if it should be presently
found that ethnicity is not strongly related to suburban
voting, attitudes, and political participation, it may
still well be that the hypotheses would be confirmed in a
nonpartisan community.

That diversity exists in Ramapo is also reflected in
terms of the various religious establishments and ethnic
communities in the town. Of the 53 churches and temples
listed in the 1970 Ramapo Town Data Book, 22 percent are
"upper-status" Protestants (Episcopal, Congregational, or
Presbyterian), while 27 percent are "lower-status" Protestant (Lutheran, Methodist, or Baptist--largely Black).

In addition, 10 percent are Catholic and 36 percent are
Jewish, including a sizable Orthodox-Chassidic community
in the Monsey-Spring Valley area. Unfortunately, no recent data exist to indicate the number of adherents to
each faith.

It is also notable that national differences exist
within the Catholic community of Ramapo. A large Italian
constituency exists in the Suffern area, while some of the
unincorporated and lesser developed localities house German and Irish contingents. It is interesting that the
older, incorporated village areas tend to house more com-
pact and homogeneous ethnic communities (Jews in the
Monsey-Spring Valley area, Italians in Suffern, Blacks
in Spring Valley proper, Germans in Sloatsberg, and
white Protestants in Sloatsberg-Hillburn). The newer
largely unincorporated locales in which the largest influx
of recent residents and widespread building has taken
place, often tend to be somewhat more heterogeneous.

Also of interest is the proximity of these various
ethnic groups. This is especially important in terms of
certain sociopolitical attitudes. Thus, if a group lives
on the border of a largely Black neighborhood, it may be
that its sensitivity to racial questions is due to its
residential locations. It should therefore be noted that
the residents living closest to the Black "hill" in Spring
Valley are largely Jewish, while Italians and Protestants
live closest to the Jewish neighborhoods. Obviously the
analysis is coarse and subject to steady change, since the
population increase from 1960 to 1970 was 118 percent according to the 1970 Ramapo Town Data Book.

It seems evident that Ramapo is a township with typical suburban affluence yet within which there is still
social and political diversity. This makes it an apt and
proper setting for the present study. To execute the
study, the following procedure was followed.

THE METHODOLOGY

A random sampling, based upon the use of a computer-
ized list of random numbers, was drawn from the 1972
Ramapo town voter registration rolls. Seven names were
chosen from each of the town's 75 electoral districts,
with a resultant number of 525 subjects for analysis. In
the event that a name was drawn of a voter who had moved,
died, or was similarly inaccessible, interviewers were instructed to first go to the house to the left and then to

the right of the one originally chosen. If the original
house was not a corner house, then a corner house was
never selected as an alternate. If the original house
was a corner house, then interviewers were instructed to
choose only a corner house as an alternate. Finally, in
the event that the original subject chosen was an apartment dweller, interviewers were instructed to try the
apartment to the left and then the one to the right of
the original but not to go to a different floor of the
building in case apartments of different value be chosen.
At no time did these instructions prove to be inadequate.
Interviewers were female college students screened by the
author and given careful instructions in the means and
the manner of carrying out survey interviews.

    Although the original sample included 525 subjects,
six were immediately dropped from the analysis because
they were nonwhite. This number was far too small to allow meaningful analysis in terms of voting, attitudes,
and interests yet interfered with a controlled analysis
of the responses of the white majority. As a result, the
final sample size was 519. The questionnaire presented
to these respondents is to be found in Appendix A and
will be analyzed shortly.

    Although the present study is intended to measure
the voting and attitudinal proclivities of groups within
the electorate rather than to predict or analyze the
town's voting patterns per se, it would be interesting to
test the representativeness of the sample. This is possible by simply comparing the electoral results of the
survey data with the actual results of the elections, as
provided by the Rockland County Board of Elections. This
test of the accuracy of the data follows.

Office	Survey Results (in percent)	Actual Results (in percent)
President	R--56.0	R--57.4
	D--38.6	D--42.6
Congressman	R--40.1	R--43.6
	D--56.8	D--56.4
State Senate	R--42.1	R--46.1
	D--52.9	D--53.9
Town Justice	R--39.4	R--42.3
	D--51.4	D--54.3
County Sheriff	R--44.4	R--49.7
	D--53.1	D--50.3

Note: R = Republican, D = Democrat.

Clearly, the survey data were quite close to the actual results. In each case, the correct winner was indicated by the survey data, which was generally within 4 percent of the actual election results. In addition, with the exception of the county sheriff election, the survey data approximated the winning margin within 4.5 percent. When it is considered that (1) the survey was taken three to six months after the election and many respondents may well have forgotten for whom they voted, especially in local elections; (2) the survey was done in the midst of a national electoral scandal of considerable proportion; and (3) respondents may have erroneously claimed to have voted for the winner after the fact, it appears that the data drew upon a representative sampling of the Ramapo electorate and can be analyzed with some confidence.

Essentially, the hypotheses earlier presented divide political activity into three classes: voting, attitudes, and interest. In addition, certain variables have been named as those traditionally studied in voter analyses. These are education, occupation, party affiliation (and its intensity), issue positions, ethnicity (and its intensity), and the voter's perceptions of the candidates. The following analysis of the questionnaire (see Appendix A) will indicate how these classes of political activity and variables were operationalized for this study.

The socioeconomic class of the respondent was ascertained through education and occupation. It is preferable to ask for occupation and education for these are variables less likely to be objectionable to the respondent than income. In addition, considering the job market of the seventies, annual earnings may not be an accurate measure of the respondent's class, particularly in the upper levels. These items were grouped by the same means used by the Rockland County Planning Board. Thus, since the median number of school years completed among residents in the town over 21, is 12.7, education was grouped into four categories: (1) non-high school graduate; (2) high school graduate; (3) some college; and (4) college graduate. Occupation was grouped into four categories as well: (1) Professional--including medical, legal, technical, and managerial occupations; (2) White Collar--including teachers, administrators, sales, and clerical personnel; (3) Skilled Labor--including craftsmen, factory operators, and transport personnel; and (4) Unskilled Labor--including domestic and service personnel.

The party affiliation of the respondent was ascertained by the respondent's own assessment, as was the strength of partisan identification, should it exist. Issue relevance and familiarity have been divided into two components: whether the voter believes issues to be relevant on the local scene, and whether he is open to the lines of communication from which he may learn of these issues. Self-assessment was used to determine subjective issue-interest. However, it is recognized that some respondents may feel that "issues" should be important though they themselves are ignorant of them. Thus, several items tested the subject's receptivity to the local media. The assumption is that one who pays little attention to the local media probably knows little about the issues on the local scene. It should also be noted that the local media is not the only form of communication from which the subjects may receive issue information. Word-of-mouth and personal interaction with friends and/or community opinion leaders may also be significant. Therefore, the frequency with which local politics is discussed with friends was also measured.

Further, in order for the voter to place significance upon the party label, the personality of the candidate, or the issues he does believe to be relevant, he must perceive there to be definite differences between the parties and/or the candidates. While it is recognized that individual elections may produce candidates for certain posts that do present the voter with an alternative, a test of the voter's general perceptions of the local scene was also employed.

The ethnic identification of the respondent has been divided into two component parts: religion and nationality. In the event that the subject was Black, the interviewer so recorded (as a result of the small number of Blacks in the sample, they were eliminated from the actual study). Nationality was not included for Jews or Protestants but was requested for Catholics. This dual component for Catholics allowed analysis of not only religious differences but also national differences within the Catholic community. In all cases the intensity of ethnic identification by the respondent's own estimation was tested and allowed analysis across ethnic lines for those subjects of stronger religious or national ties.

Once the respondent was categorized according to his socioeconomic, political, demographic, and interest characteristics, it was possible to compare the impact of several variables upon the vote. The electoral choices

of the subjects was ascertained by their responses to the
two ballots included in the questionnaire. Ballot A (see
Appendix A) was a re-creation of the 1972 ballot for
Ramapo, including national, state, and local elections.
Ballot B was a proposed ballot for the 1973 local elections in Ramapo and was compiled with the help of the
chairmen of both local parties. It should be noted that
each ballot included a good distribution of ethnic candidates among both parties. Ballot A contains a Republican
Italian (Codispotti) as well as a Democratic Italian
(Roselli), as does Ballot B (Capuano and Balsalmo respectively). This pattern holds true for Jews, Irish and
German Catholics, and Protestants as well. The subject
was asked to treat the ballot as they did in November--
or as they would if today were election day. This permitted comparison and correlation to determine which variables were most important and to delineate trends among
the voters.

The general policy orientations of the respondents
were ascertained by his responses to items constructed to
test for the following issues: residential integration,
drug abuse, economics, planning and race (the placements
of high-rise apartments is an issue of constant concern
to the residents of the town because of the fear that
such structures would mean increased urbanization, influx
of lower-income and Black residents, and a lowering of
property values), education and economics (the largest
single tax item in Ramapo is for education and equals
some $11.00 per $100 of assessment), welfare, and law and
order. These issue-areas were chosen with the help of
the chairmen of both local political parties as the most
important issues facing the local candidates in the 1973
elections. Since it is difficult to determine which posi-
tion on any of these rather complex issues is the more
liberal or conservative, it was decided that each would
be treated separately rather than be scaled cumulatively
in order to label subjectively the respondent more "liberal" or "conservative." Therefore, each response was
correlated to each independent variable individually to
determine which factors were most influential in each
issue-area. Attitudes were also used as independent
variables in correspondence with the vote. This permitted analysis of the impact of given crucial issues on
the vote, as well as the socioeconomic and demographic
variables earlier mentioned.

Interest in local politics was operationally defined
by two elements: nonvoting and exposure to local channels

of information and news. To determine the extent of non-voting among subjects, the respondent was only asked about his voting activity in 1972, because it is unreasonable to expect him to recall whether he has voted in specific elections in past years. Further, a general question--such as "How often do you vote?"--would accomplish little, for few respondents would admit to voting rarely, especially in a middle-class suburb. In addition, since 1972 was a presidential election year in which 85.5 percent of the eligible voters in Ramapo actually did vote, it may be assumed that the respondent does not vote regularly if he admits to not voting in 1972.

In addition, several items were used to test the respondent's exposure to local information sources. If the respondent indicated little exposure to the local media in regard to local affairs, despite the fact that he voted in 1972, a new reason for separating local from national affairs may surface. It would be fair to assume that his activity at the polls is motivated by other than local interest, since he is not exposed to local affairs.

These several items regarding local media were not cumulatively scaled to determine which were the more or less interested voters. This was because many of the items may operate independently of each other. For example, it is possible for a respondent to be a regular and careful follower of local politics in the local press (and therefore well aware of local issues), though he has little time for local radio (which ends its broadcasting at 6:00 p.m.). A cumulative scale would hide this fact by rating a subject for his responses in all areas relevant to local media. Therefore, these items were evaluated individually of each other.

Once the level and intensity of the subject's participation and interest in local politics were determined, these items were related to the various other items regarding the subject's socioeconomic, attitudinal, and political characteristics.

This then is the context within which the present study was undertaken. The intent is to gauge the importance of ethnicity in the suburban political arena. The setting for this research is a typical suburban township in the New York City area, the Town of Ramapo in Rockland County. Socioeconomically, the area is affluent and upper-status, not unlike other suburban communities in the region. Politically, there seems to be some diversity in terms of party affiliation and voting habits, as indicated by the registration rolls and recent results in both national and local elections.

The method used to study this area is based upon
random survey analysis and standard statistical tests.
Respondents were questioned in three distinct political
areas: voting habits, attitudes, and interest-participation. In the chapters that follow, each of these three
areas will be treated separately, as dependent variables.
This will allow a clear view of the impact of each of the
other factors in each area. A following chapter will
then attempt to develop a causal scheme (based upon the
foregoing results), which will clarify the progression of
factors that lead ultimately to the vote. A final, con-
cluding chapter will attempt to evaluate the results in
terms of the present scholarly literature and indicate
what, if any, new conclusions seem to emerge from the
data.

The first dependent variable in our analysis of the importance of ethnicity in the suburbs is the voting record of suburban residents. These were reported by respondents three to six months after the 1972 election. Prior to analyzing the data and comparing it with the hypotheses earlier presented, it would be well to outline briefly the major themes in the scholarly literature relevant to ethnicity and suburban voting.

AN OVERVIEW

Prior to 1960, it was believed that suburbia was the haven of staunch Republicanism. This was attributed to one of two factors: (1) Conversion--This thesis postulated that central-city dwellers, upon their movement to the suburbs, changed their political allegiance to accommodate to their new surroundings. In this sense, the suburbs were termed "political Jordans from which Democrats emerged Republicans."[1] (2) Transplantation--In this version, the suburban move was looked upon as a correlate, rather than cause, of Republican voting trends. Both the move and the greater Republicanism were attributed to the more significant factor of upward social mobility.[2]

The 1960 election, in which the Democrat Kennedy received some 49 percent of the suburban vote, motivated a series of sociopolitical studies which led to alternative theories regarding suburban electoral behavior. It was postulated that there existed working- and lower-class suburbs, as well as lower-class areas within suburbs. It was also argued that political diversity could be found within suburbs, and that given suburbs were often more politically similar to their own central-city areas than to other suburbs.[3]

Although new hypotheses have been forwarded regarding suburban politics, one factor which has been conspicuous for its absence in these formulations is ethnicity. Analysts have either dismissed its importance out of hand[4] or have dealt with it as an entity unto itself, without considering its importance in the political realm.[5] Those few writers who have dealt with ethnicity in the suburbs have done so in a speculative fashion, leaving the empirical tests of their hypotheses for others to attempt.[6] Equally, those studies that have dealt with ethnicity in empirical-political terms have been rooted in urban centers or national samples.[7]

There may be, however, reason to believe that ethnicity will play an important role in the electoral choices of suburban residents.

The conversion-transplantation controversy may well have proven irrelevant in terms of the change of political allegiance. However, perhaps the same factors assumed to cause a Republican shift are in fact operative in weakening party affiliation and permitting other variables to surface. Perhaps party loyalties felt in the city are not felt as strongly, if at all, in the suburbs. Further, those loyalties still felt may have their greatest impact in national elections, due to their high visibility and the great excitement they generate. More local elections may be the most likely to be affected by the influences of conversion-transplantation, in the sense that old partisan loyalties will be most weakened.

Some support for this hypothesis may be derived from a number of prior studies. It has been found that in the absence of party labels, either in nonpartisan elections or "controlled" survey ballots, voters tend to choose candidates of their own (the voters') ethnic group to a significant degree.[8] If this is the voter's response in a "no-party" election, it may also be an indication of his response in an election in which the party label means little to him. If indeed partisan affiliation of all types is weakened and, in situations in which the party label is absent (or assumedly irrelevant), voters tend to choose candidates based upon their ethnic identification, it may be expected that in local suburban elections, voters will choose those candidates whom they perceive to be of their (the voters') ethnic group.

It is also significant to note that it has been found that members of the same ethnic group tend to live together in the suburbs. When the degree of ethnic residential segregation in the suburbs was compared to that of the cities, for the period 1930-50, no significant differences emerged.[9] Perhaps this implies an ethnic social structure which serves many of the suburbanites' needs just as it may have in the city.[10] It may also indicate that those who abandon the cities seek "suburbs of like-minded and like-situated people."[11] In the extreme, this may result in "suburban districts which have become as heavily Jewish or Italian or Irish as were the ghettos of 'Little Italies' or 'New Erins.'"[12]

It has further been found that attendance at religious services and participation in religious communal activities tends to rise among second- and third-generation Americans in the suburbs.[13] Though it has been indicated that such participation serves more a social than spiritual need, it may be inferred that not only do ethnic enclaves exist in the suburbs but to the extent that ethnicity may be defined as religion, suburbanites actively identify with their ethnic (religious) communities. It is not unreasonable, therefore, to assume that voters who may have consciously sought, resided in, and participated in a given type of community will be influenced by these surroundings at the polls. It may be expected that members of different ethnic groups will vote differently as a result.

The foregoing analysis has served as the basis for the assumptions regarding the possible strength of ethnicity in the suburbs. Essentially, it has been argued that because of the general tendency to weaken the several other socioeconomic and demographic variables in the suburbs, ethnicity--defined by religious affiliation and national identity--may replace them as a major determinant of the suburban vote. Generally, this relationship may be more pronounced in local elections than in those of national standing. To add scientific precision to the analysis, this proposition has been stated in more direct and succinct language:

1. Ethnicity will be more important than any other variable in voter choice for local suburban elections.

- Ethnicity will be more important than party affiliation, social class, issue positions, interest levels, or candidate perception.
- Members of similar ethnic groups will have a greater tendency to vote for candidates whom they perceive to be of their own group (as recognizable by the candidate's last name) than any others, in local elections.

- Members of similar ethnic groups will tend to vote similarly irrespective of the ethnic identification of the candidate.

As is clearly implied in the hypothesis, the influence of ethnicity on voting may be construed in two ways: People of the same ethnic group tend to vote alike; people tend to vote for candidates whom they perceive to be of their (the voters') ethnic group. Since the analysis of these two points requires different empirical tests, the respective data will be presented separately.

DO ETHNICS VOTE ALIKE?

In order to study the first of the two points implied by the hypothesis, members of the same ethnic group vote alike, data gathered from the ballot section of the survey questionnaire will be used. If the hypothesis is correct, then significant differences between the voting habits of the various ethnic groups should emerge. Further, the strength of these relationships (as measured by the magnitude of the contingency coefficient--value of C) should be greater than any others. To test the significance of the relationship between ethnicity and the vote, five elections were chosen from those reported in the data. These elections were chosen from each level of government: (1) National--presidential and congressional elections; (2) State--state senate election; (3) County--county sheriff election; and (4) Town--town justice election. (These were chosen because other state elections did not include the entire town, while other local elections were merely projections for 1973. As a result, large numbers of respondents expressed doubt at these other choices and hesitated in answering.) It is first necessary to ascertain whether ethnicity is a significant variable at all in suburban voting, and thence to determine its comparative importance to other sociopolitical variables. Ethnicity, operationally defined by religion for white Protestants and Jews, and further defined by national background for white Catholics, can now be analyzed in the context of voting. The following present the data for the presidential and congressional elections, related to religion. (In order to eliminate zeroes and facilitate the use of the statistical tests, "Other" and "No Response" categories have been eliminated.)

Relationship between religion and the presidential vote.

24

Religion	Nixon (R)	McGovern (D)
Protestant (n = 86)	75.6%	24.4%
Catholic (n = 156)	71.8	28.2
Jewish (n = 197)	52.3	47.7

$x^2 = 18.57$ P = .005 2df
C = .2128

Relationship between religion and the vote for congressman.

Religion	Gilman (R)	Dow (D)
Protestant (n = 86)	52.3%	47.7%
Catholic (n = 155)	52.3	47.7
Jewish (n = 198)	31.8	68.1

$x^2 = 18.57$ P = .005 2df
C = .2014

It may first be noted that members of different ethnic groups who happen to live in the suburbs do vote differently to a significant degree. In the presidential election, Protestants were most favorable to Nixon and Catholics slightly less favorable to his candidacy. Jews, though a majority of those responding did not vote Republican, were far more favorable toward the Democratic candidate than the other two groups. This is much the same in the case of the congressional election. An equal majority of Protestants and Catholics (52.3 percent of each) voted for the Republican Gilman, while a large majority of the Jewish respondents (68.1 percent) voted for his Democratic competitor, John Dow. In these terms, it may be tentatively said that the general omission of ethnicity in prior analyses of suburban voting patterns in national elections may have been in error. The data also permit similar analysis of the relationship between national background of Catholics and these two elections. If ethnicity, defined by religion, proves to be significant, it should be interesting to see if the same proves true of national background. The following present this data.

Relationship between nationality and the vote for president (among Catholic respondents).

Nationality	Nixon (R)	McGovern (D)
Irish (n = 33)	66.6%	33.3%
Italian (n = 70)	77.1	22.9
German (n = 21)	71.4	28.6

$x^2 = 1.30$ NS 2df

Relationship between nationality and the vote for congressman (among Catholic respondents).

Nationality	Gilman(R)	Dow(D)
Irish (n = 33)	54.5%	45.5%
Italian (n = 70)	58.6	41.4
German (n = 22)	59.1	40.9

x^2 = .17   NS 2df

As the data indicate, at least in relation to federal elections, Catholics do not differ among themselves by nationality. It may be noted, however, that the Irish are somewhat more favorable toward the Democratic candidates than are other Catholic groups. Although inference is strictly limited by the insignificance of the data, the findings may be related to the oft mentioned tie between the Irish voters and the Democratic party. This tie has been attributed to the role played by the Democratic urban machines in aiding and courting the Irish immigrant during the period of early settlement.[14] Indeed, the very insignificance of the data may indicate that the Irish have lost this Democratic commitment and become not much different from other Catholic voters.[15]

The prior tables indicated the significance of ethnicity at the national and congressional levels. As has been argued in Chapter 1, much of the electoral analysis of the suburbs has dealt with national elections, and therefore it may be possible that certain variables not generally present in national elections, but of importance in local elections, have been glossed over. It has been hypothesized that ethnicity may well be such a variable. If the premise that the importance of ethnicity will increase in more local elections is correct, then it can be expected that not only will ethnicity be significant in local elections but its contingency coefficient (C) should be higher than it was in the federal elections just studied.

Relationship between religion and the vote for state senator.

Religion	Ackerson(R)	Athens(D)
Protestant (n = 81)	45.7%	54.3%
Catholic (n = 148)	54.1	45.9
Jewish (n = 193)	35.8	64.2

x^2 = 11.48   P = .005
C = .1628

Relationship between religion and the vote for county sheriff.

Religion	Lindemann (R)	Shea (D)
Protestant (n = 79)	49.4%	50.6%
Catholic (n = 149)	54.4	45.6
Jewish (n = 192)	33.3	66.6

x^2 = 16.26   P = .005 2df
C = .1931

Relationship between religion and the vote for town justice.

Religion	Codispotti (R)	Stanger (D)
Protestant (n = 75)	52.0%	48.0%
Catholic (n = 150)	56.7	43.3
Jewish (n = 188)	30.9	69.1

x^2 = 24.89   P = .005 2df
C = .2387

As the data clearly indicate, religion is a significant variable at every electoral level. Similar to the previous findings, Jewish voters tend to be highly Democratic, much more so than voters of any other religious persuasion. Protestants were rather evenly divided between Republican and Democratic candidates at all electoral levels except the presidential, in which they gave Nixon a 75.6 percent majority. This may indicate both the great strength of the Nixon candidacy and the unimpressive length of his coattails, for Protestant respondents. It appears that for the Protestant voter, Richard Nixon's victory was largely a personal one and not a partisan one. Catholics were most consistent in their voting and gave electoral majorities to all Republican candidates, although the margin of victory given to Nixon by Catholics (71.8 percent) was by far the largest.

Also of interest are the various values of C. The initial belief that ethnicity would play a greater role in more local elections than in national elections has been generally confirmed, in the case of religion. As the following data indicate, this does not prove to be the case.

Relationship between nationality and the vote for state senator (for Catholic respondents).

Nationality	Ackerson (R)	Athens (D)
Irish (n = 30)	46.7%	53.3%
Italian (n = 67)	61.2	38.8
German (n = 21)	42.9	57.1

x^2 = 3.10 NS 2df

Relationship between nationality and the vote for county sheriff (for Catholic respondents).

Nationality	Lindemann (R)	Shea (D)
Irish (n = 30)	50.0%	50.0%
Italian (n = 68)	64.7	35.3
German (n = 21)	38.1	61.9

x^2 = 5.26 NS 2df

Relationship between nationality and the vote for town justice (for Catholic respondents).

Nationality	Codispotti (R)	Stanger (D)
Irish (n = 31)	51.6%	48.4%
Italian (n = 70)	64.3	25.7
German (n = 20)	50.0	50.0

x^2 = 3.61 NS 2df

It seems from the data that to the extent that ethnicity is a significant variable in suburban voting, it
is defined by religion and not by national background.
Indeed, even there the values of C were not very high. In
no instance was there a significant relationship between
nationality, for Catholics, and the vote. Nevertheless,
a few remarks regarding the data are in order. While no
significant differences emerge when all three Catholic
nationality groups are compared with each other, it is
still possible that individual groups differ from all
other Catholics. For example, while the relationship
among Irish, Italian, and German Catholic respondents may
not be significant in their choice of a state senate candidate, it may still be that a comparison between Irish
voters and all other Catholics will yield a significant
difference. This possibility seems most likely in more
local elections. At the presidential and congressional
levels, groups did not differ from each other by more
than 6 percent. A quick glance at the data regarding the
three more local elections will show the reader that

considerable differences separate the three groups, especially the Germans (who gave large majorities to the
Democratic candidates) and the Italians (who gave similar
majorities to the Republican local candidates). If significant relationships emerge for certain groups but not
for others, it may be that nationality does play a role in
voting, albeit only for certain Catholic groups. These
relationships were tested and the results are given below.

Chi-square values for individual Catholic nationality
groups in three local elections, 1 df.

Nationality	State Senate	County Sheriff	Town Justice
Irish	.94	.64	.85
Italian	3.03	4.55[a]	2.15
German	1.33	3.42	.75

[a]Significant at .05

As the data indicate, no significant relationship
surfaces when individual Catholic nationality groups are
compared with all other Catholics, except for Italians in
the county sheriff elections. It is apparent that nationality does not define ethnicity for the Catholic
voter. Rather, the political salience of ethnicity is
only significant in terms of religion. It must finally
be noted that what is being tested here is statistical
significance, rather than political significance. Therefore, while the chi-square values may not be high enough
to permit statistical inference from the data, this does
not mean that the differences between Catholic nationality
groups is not sufficient to have a political impact on
electoral results, candidate appeal, strategy, or political style. Indeed, casual discussions with local party
leaders and candidates have indicated that the "Italian"
vote especially is looked upon as a viable political entity independent from the vote of Catholics generally.
In fact, the term is used often and quite loosely. The
present data do not permit such inference, however, and
must be limited to tests of statistical significance only.

DO ETHNICS VOTE FOR FELLOW-ETHNICS?

The previous section dealt only with one aspect of
ethnic influence on suburban voting patterns: the proposition that members of the same ethnic group vote alike.
This was found to be the case, to a significant degree,

only when ethnicity was defined as religious group membership. A second possible influence brings into play the
ethnic group membership of the candidate, to the extent
that it is recognizable from the candidate's name. This
second influence implies that there should be a significant difference between the general voting habits of a
given group and their choice when a fellow-ethnic is on
the ballot. To test this aspect of the hypothesis, the
mean Democratic vote of each ethnic group (M.D.V.) was
compared with the mean vote of each group when a fellow
ethnic ran on the Democratic ticket. This latter score
was termed mean Democratic vote-ethnic (M.D.V.-E.). This
data is presented below.

Comparison of M.D.V. with mean Democratic vote for
ethnic candidate by religion.

Religion	M.D.V.	M.D.V.-E.
Protestant (n = 91)	39.90%	41.52%
Catholic (n = 169)	35.65	34.08
Jewish (n = 208)	55.44	62.50

x^2 = 2.69 NS 2df

Most evident from this data is the fact that there is
no significant difference between the voting habits of
each religious group, generally, and their choices when a
fellow group member is on the ticket. In fact, in the
case of the Catholics, the mean vote is slightly lower
when a Catholic was the Democratic candidate!

The converse, however, must also be tested. It may
be that there is no difference in the Democratic vote
whether or not an ethnic is on the ticket, but the effect
will manifest itself in a negative form, that is, when an
ethnic is the Republican candidate. Thus it may be expected that the mean negative ethnic Democratic vote
(M.D.V. in all those elections in which a fellow-ethnic
ran as a Republican = M.D.V. Neg.-E.) will be significantly lower than the M.D.V. for each group.

Comparison of M.D.V. with Democratic vote when Republican was ethnic candidate (by religion).

Religion	M.D.V.	M.D.V. Neg.-E.
Protestant (n = 91)	39.90%	35.75%
Catholic (n = 169)	35.65	36.44
Jewish (n = 208)	55.44	53.86

x^2 = 3.65 NS 2df

Clearly, no such significant relationship exists.
In addition, while both the Jewish and Protestant vote
differ in expected direction, the Catholic vote runs counter to expectations, as before. Religion has an apparent
influence on the suburban vote only so far as its members
vote alike. However, its influence does not seem to extend to increasing the vote of its candidate-members.

Although ethnicity has also been defined in terms of
national background, this variable did not prove significant in terms of influencing the vote, in the earlier
section. For example, members of various Catholic nationality groups did not vote similarly to a significant
degree. It is possible, however, that the effect of nationality is to motivate group members to vote for others
of the same group. The same comparative tests as above
may be used to analyze this possibility. The following
table presents the first of these tests: a comparison
between the M.D.V. of each group and their M.D.V.-E.

Comparison of M.D.V. of Catholics with M.D.V.-E., by
nationality.

Nationality	M.D.V.	M.D.V.-E.
Irish (n = 35)	38.72%	41.93%
Italian (n = 74)	29.96	24.30
German (n = 26)	36.02	38.46

$x^2 = 3.09$

It is again evident that ethnicity does not affect
the vote in a significant way. Further, while Irish and
German respondents vary in the expected direction, the
mean Democratic vote for ethnic candidates of Italian
voters is actually lower than their mean Democratic vote.
Once again, however, this only tests the positive manifestations of the hypothesis. It is still possible that
ethnic voters will be more likely to choose a Republican
fellow ethnic than just any Republican. The relationship
of the M.D.V. with the mean Democratic vote when a fellow-
ethnic is the Republican candidate (mean negative-ethnic
Democratic vote) is compared below.

Comparison of M.D.V. of Catholics with Democratic
vote when ethnic candidate was Republican, by nationality.

Nationality	M.D.V.	M.D.V. Neg.-E.
Irish (n = 35)	38.72%	32.9%
Italian (n = 74)	29.96	33.8
German (n = 26)	36.02	50.0

$x^2 = 7.75$ P = .025 2df

The results of this test are most interesting. A significant relationship has emerged. It is, however, largely opposite from the direction required to confirm the hypothesis. While the results are in the expected direction for the Irish voters, that is, there is a lower M.D.V. in those elections in which the Republican candidate was Irish, the relationships for the Italian and especially the German voters are quite the opposite. In these cases, the voters chose Democratic candidates more often precisely when the Republican was a fellow-ethnic. This may indicate that ethnicity had a negative influence upon the voters--it influenced their vote insofar as it convinced them to vote against a fellow-ethnic. It is equally possible that ethnicity played no role at all in the decision, and the choice was made for reasons other than the candidate's ethnic identity. In general, it seems clear that the impact of the ethnic identity of the candidate--as identified by his name--is negligible and the hypothesis is not confirmed.

In sum, it is apparent that ethnicity in general is not a very influential variable in determining the suburban vote. The present data indicate that ethnicity is found to be significant in relation to the vote only in certain limited instances. These are:
- When defined as religion alone;
- Only insofar as members of the same religious group vote alike;
- At all levels of government, though more strongly at the presidential and town levels.

It is clearly not significant when it is defined as membership of a specific nationality group, for Catholics. No significant relationships exist either among the three nationality groups studied (German, Irish, or Italian Catholics) or between any one of them and all others. Ethnicity is also not significant when it is defined as the tendency for members of a particular group to choose candidates of their own ethnic group.

THE ROLE OF OTHER VARIABLES

It is now possible to test whether ethnicity (herein defined as religion) is more significant than any other variable in relation to the electoral choices of the respondents. This can be done by presenting other variables found to be significant and comparing their contingency coefficients (C) with those of religion for the appropriate elections.

The data clearly indicate that ethnicity-religion was not the most significant of variables in relation to the vote. Both in terms of strength of association and in terms of consistency, two variables were found to be more significant. These are the respondent's party affiliation and his attitude regarding residential segregation. Once again, it will be convenient to look first at the results for national elections, presidential and congressional. The following present the national electoral results related to the respondent's party affiliation.

Relationship between party affiliation and the vote for president.

Party	Nixon (R)	McGovern (D)
Republican (n = 154)	95.5%	4.5%
Democrat (n = 269)	38.7	61.3

$x^2 = 133.21$ P = .001 1df
C = .4893

Relationship between party affiliation and vote for congressman.

Party	Gilman (R)	Dow (D)
Republican (n = 154)	77.9%	22.1%
Democrat (n = 270)	21.1	78.9

$x^2 = 130.15$ P = .001 1df
C = .4847

It is quite evident that a strong relationship exists between party affiliation and the vote. Virtually all those who claimed to be Republicans voted for Nixon, while a large majority of those claiming to be Democrats voted for McGovern (61.3 percent). Similarly, the overwhelming majority of Republican respondents voted for the Republican congressional candidate (Gilman) while virtually the same percentage of Democratic respondents voted for the Democratic congressional candidate (Dow).

In addition, the value of C for these two relationships are .4893 and .4847 respectively. These are far higher than the coefficients found for religion in relation to these two elections (.2128 and .2014 respectively) and consequently imply a much stronger relationship. The impact of ethnicity is relatively weak when compared to party affiliation as a variable influencing the suburban vote in federal elections. However, it has been noted that there may exist a qualitative difference between the voting habits of suburbanites in national elections and their electoral choices at the local level. In fact, it was found that the relationship between religion and the vote was strongest at the most local level. It has been conjectured that this increased strength might have been at the expense of such "high-visibility" election variables as partisan affiliation. If this is the case, it may be expected that the C values for the relationship between party affiliation and the local vote will be lower than they were for federal level elections. As the following indicate, this was not the case.

Relationship between party affiliation and the vote for state senator.

Party	Ackerson (R)	Athens (D)
Republican (n = 141)	77.3%	22.7%
Democrat (n = 264)	22.0	78.0

x^2 = 116.14 P = .001 1df
C = .4722

Relationship between party affiliation and the vote for sheriff.

Party	Lindemann (R)	Shea (D)
Republican (n = 139)	75.5%	24.5%
Democrat (n = 264)	23.1	76.9

x^2 = 103.34 P = .001 1df
C = .4517

Relationship between party affiliation and the vote for town justice.

Party	Codispotti (R)	Stanger (D)
Republican (n = 140)	81.4%	18.6%
Democrat (n = 262)	21.8	78.2

x^2 = 132.91 P = .001
C = .4984

Quite clearly, party affiliation plays an extremely important role in the vote at all levels. The value of C has remained above .45 for each election, and the strongest relationship was found to be the most local election, town justice. This latter relationship yielded a C value of .4984. This runs counter to the expected decrease of the importance of party affiliation at the local level.

In addition, two further notes are in order. It was earlier mentioned that a strong school of thought held suburbia to be the bastion of Republicanism.[16] The above results indicate that this thesis does not apply to Ramapo. Not only did Democrats receive electoral majorities there in 1972, but a majority of those interviewed (54.8 percent) identified themselves as Democrats. It should be noted, however, that this effect may be the result of Democratic influences from New York City.

This leads to yet another intriguing inference suggested by the data. It has also been asserted that the suburbs are an area of no clear political culture.[17] Alternately, it is suggested that in the suburbs there exists a form of "no-party politics" and "conscious nonpartisanship."[18] Apparently these assertions are equally inapplicable to Ramapo in 1972, where the data imply the existence of a very sophisticated and complex political culture quite partisan in nature. At every electoral level, an overwhelming percentage of Republican voters chose the Republican candidate, while the opposite was true of a similar percentage of Democratic voters. It seems that in 1972 Ramapo voters identified themselves with a political party and then acted upon that identification at the polls.

A second variable of less importance than party affiliation, but of greater importance than religion, was found to be voter attitude toward residential segregation. Subjects' attitudes were tested by their responses to a series of statements dealing with issues of general and local political importance. Among these was included the following: "I see nothing wrong with Black people moving onto this block." This statement was designed to test the respondent's attitudes regarding residential segregation. That this issue is of great import to suburban residents generally has been pointed out often.[19] The following indicate that the issue is also one which has considerable electoral impact. ("Agree Strongly" and "Disagree Strongly" categories have been eliminated and combined with "Agree" and "Disagree" respectively to facilitate use of the chi-square statistic.)

Relationship between respondent's attitude regarding residential segregation and the vote for president. Statement: "I see nothing wrong with Black people moving onto this block."

Response	Nixon (R)	McGovern (D)
Agree (n = 184)	46.7%	53.3%
No Opinion (n = 150)	64.0	36.0
Disagree (n = 136)	82.4	17.6

$x^2 = 42.54$ P = .001 2df   C = .2881

Relationship between respondent's attitude regarding residential segregation and the vote for congressman. Statement: "I see nothing wrong with Black people moving onto this block."

Response	Gilman (R)	Dow (D)
Agree (n = 186)	29.6%	70.4%
No Opinion (n = 151)	51.0	49.0
Disagree (n = 133)	53.4	46.6

$x^2 = 23.92$ P = .001 2df   C = .2200

It is apparent that a significant relationship exists between the subject's electoral choices and his attitude regarding residential segregation. Not inconsistent with their stated positions in the areas of desegregation and civil rights, the Republican presidential and congressional candidates received their strongest support from those voters who were least tolerant toward residential integration. Conversely, those who displayed the most tolerant racial attitude were most favorably disposed to the Democratic candidates.

In addition, the C values for the above two relationships are also of note. The association of the respondent's attitude toward residential segregation with the presidential election yielded a coefficient of .2881, while the similar relationship with the congressional election yielded a .2200 coefficient. These indicate a stronger relationship between the above variables than was found to exist between religion and the vote, in which the coefficients were .2128 and .2014 respectively. It seems apparent that in elections at the federal level, religion is less important than the respondent's racial attitude, as well as his party affiliation.

In earlier analysis, it was speculated that while party affiliation might be important to the suburban voter in high-visibility elections such as the presidential election, it might have less impact in more local elections. This hypothesis was not confirmed in the case of party affiliation where the most local election, town justice, actually had the highest C value.

It is difficult to apply this hypothesis to the area
of racial attitude. On the one hand, it may be that the
same logic applied to the party affiliation analysis (and
unconfirmed by empirical tests here) may apply. In this
version, racial attitude would hold importance only in
high-visibility elections, because it is only in such
elections that the positions of the candidates would have
sufficient exposure to influence the perceptions and actions of the voters. In the absence of such great exposure, the attitude of the voter, though still present to
be sure, would have little opportunity to surface in any
electorally salient manner.

By the same token, however, it may be that the amount
of exposure a candidate has will have little to do with
this aspect of the voter's perceptions. Those who have
found that race and residential segregation, especially
the latter, are very important issues to the suburban
voter have postulated that fear of urbanization, central-
ization, large-scale development, and down-zoning are in
many senses to be equated with fear of Black encroachment.
Such analysts have argued that for the suburbanite (1) the
move from the city may well have been motivated by the
"advance" of the Black resident into white neighborhoods;
(2) the most important function of suburban government is
excluding undesirables, which "to the suburban residents
of northern industrial cities . . . probably means
Negro. . . ."; and (3) the fear of residential integration extends to renters as well as homeowners, raising
serious questions regarding the assumed relationship between intolerance and the fear of lowered property values.[20] If the assumptions of these writers are correct,
then it may be that the issue of residential segregation
is important enough for the voter to discover the positions of local candidates even in low-visibility elections.

In addition, the discussion thus far has only considered the possibility that the relationship between
racial attitude and the vote is a direct one. It is also
possible that party affiliation intervenes in the relationship and gives the voter his cues as to which candidate will likely have given attitudes in important issue-
areas. It is possible that religion may play a similar
role.

Therefore, it is quite difficult to conjecture about
the impact of visibility on the relationship between the
vote and the respondent's racial attitude. The following
present the actual results when racial attitude was related to the three more local elections.

Relationship between respondent's attitude regarding residential segregation and the vote for state senate. Statement: "I see nothing wrong with Black people moving onto this block."

Response	Ackerson (R)	Athens (D)
Agree (n = 180)	36.7%	63.3%
No Opinion (n = 146)	41.8	58.2
Disagree (n = 125)	56.8	43.2

x^2 = 12.25   P = .001 2df   C = .1646

Relationship between respondent's attitude regarding residential segregation and the vote for county sheriff. Statement: "I see nothing wrong with Black people moving onto this block."

Response	Lindemann (R)	Shea (D)
Agree (n = 183)	32.2%	67.8%
No Opinion (n = 146)	44.5	55.5
Disagree (n = 121)	62.8	37.2

x^2 = 27.57   P = .001 2df   C = .2402

Relationship between respondent's attitude regarding residential segregation and the vote for town justice. Statement: "I see nothing wrong with Black people moving onto this block."

Response	Codispotti (R)	Stanger (D)
Agree (n = 176)	29.5%	70.5%
No Opinion (n = 143)	45.5	54.5
Disagree (n = 123)	65.9	34.1

x^2 = 38.62   P = .001 2df   C = .2835

As the data show, there is a significant relationship between the voter's racial attitude and his vote at all levels. As was the case for the presidential and congressional elections, those whose attitude toward residential segregation was more tolerant tended to choose the Democratic candidate, while those with a more exclusive attitude were more likely to choose the Republican candidate at all levels.

In addition, as the contingency coefficients indicate, the relationship was virtually as strong at the most local level as it was at the presidential level. The C value in the relationship between racial attitude and the presidential vote was C = .2881; in the relationship with the vote for town justice it was C = .2835. It should be noted that--as was the case in the relationships between the vote and party affiliation and between the vote and religion--the value of C drops at the intermediary levels, the state and county elections. It then increases at the town level.

In fact, the similarity in the activity of the C value in relation to all three variables under discussion --religion, party affiliation, and racial attitude--merits brief analysis. As has been noted (pages 34-35), the value of C tends to be highest in the presidential elections and lowers progressively in congressional and state elections. It then rises in the county elections and reaches a point approximately as high as its start at the town level. This activity is presented graphically in Figure 3.1.

FIGURE 3.1

Comparison of the Activity of C in Relation to
Religion, Party Affiliation, and Racial
Attitude in Five Suburban Elections

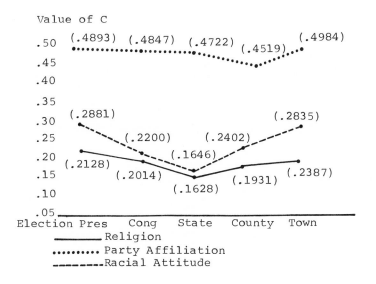

As the graph indicates, the resultant curve in each instance resembles a U. This pattern is most discernible in the case of racial attitude. It is somewhat less so in the case of party affiliation, where the effects of partisanship seem to have been quite consistent at all electoral levels. In addition, although the pattern is still discernible in relation to partisanship, it is also notable that in the case of party affiliation the C value reaches its nadir at the county level rather than at the state level, as was the case with the other two variables.

Although the present data do not allow definitive analysis of this interesting effect, a possible explanation may be suggested. It may be that presidential and town elections are the most important of all elections to the voter. Presidential elections--because of the role of the media--are given considerable publicity and therefore have high visibility. Those variables most influential in the voter's electoral decision will be most likely to have an impact upon such an election because of the attention the voter is likely to give such high-visibility affairs. Thus the three variables most consistently related to the vote in the present study tend to relate most strongly at the presidential level.

While the town elections obviously do not gain as much coverage as national elections, they may have certain properties which make them comparable. It may be that local elections in the particular locality are given much publicity. A string of local newspapers as well as local radio stations devote much time and coverage to news and affairs of a local nature. In addition, this news is often conveyed during the same radio time spots or in the same sections of the local newspapers as the national news. It may therefore be that news of a local nature is absorbed by local citizens to about the same degree as national news. Local news may be as related to the electoral decision and those variables most influential in it as national news.

Further, local elections may have an added property which would increase their importance to the local resident. Precisely because they are local, they are much closer to the voter. Their implications are more immediate to him and their ramifications more direct. He may, therefore, view the local election in the same context as he does the national election; that is, the same variables that go into his national "electoral perspective" will also be relevant to the local scene.

The same may not be true of elections at the intermediary level: state and county. Here local media may
not be as comprehensive in its coverage precisely because
state or county news is neither as immediate as local news
nor as "important" as national news. Similarly, state and
county elections are not as obviously or directly related
to the lives of local residents as are local elections,
and they do not "seem" as important as national elections.
Therefore those variables that comprise the voter's "electoral perspective" at the national or local level will not
be quite so influential at the intermediary level.

Finally, it must be noted that this analysis is not
meant to imply an absolute or extreme relationship between
the variables which influence the vote and the electoral
level. Rather, as the electoral level moves farther from
the presidential, the strength of the relationships de-
cline. Thus the C values for the congressional elections
are generally lower than the presidential but higher than
those at the state level, and so on. Obviously, the above
can only be suggestive and requires more study and analysis.[21]

ETHNICITY AND THE SUBURBAN VOTE:
A SUMMARY ANALYSIS

A number of interesting results have surfaced in the
data of the voting habits of Ramapo citizens. It is first
evident that the earlier hypothesis regarding the importance of ethnicity will have to be severely modified. It
was first postulated that ethnicity, defined as religion
and nationality for Catholics, would be the most important
variable to the suburban voter. This hypothesis was
divided into two areas: the response of the voters when
a fellow-ethnic was on the ballot, and the similarities
in the habits of voters professing similar ethnic identities. It was found that:

1. In almost no instance is nationality a significant factor to the Catholic voter, whether each of the
three nationality groups being studied (Irish, Italian,
and German) were tested against each other or each was
tested against all other Catholics;

2. Members of an ethnic group do not vote for
fellow-ethnics to any significant degree;

3. Respondents of similar religious affiliation do
tend to vote alike to a significant degree;

41

4. The most important variable in relation to the
vote is the voter's party affiliation;

5. A second variable, more important than religion
but less important than party affiliation, is the respondent's attitude regarding residential segregation;

6. All three variables were found to be significant
at every electoral level and as significant at the most
local level as at the presidential level, with a lag at
the state and county level.

A note here is in order regarding the issue of association and causality. The statistical tests being employed here--chi-square and C--indicate the existence of
a significant relationship and its intensity. They do
not, however, indicate the direction of the relationship.
Therefore, if one finds that a voter's attitude corre-
sponds significantly with the way he votes, it is difficult to determine which is influencing which or, indeed,
if both are being influenced by a third factor. In the
present instance--the relationship between a voter's racial attitude and his vote--it is possible that voters
with less tolerant racial attitudes therefore choose Republican candidates. It is also possible that voters who
are attracted to Republican candidates for other reasons--
foreign policy positions, economic positions, "sincerity,"
looks, and so forth--are influenced by their (the candidates') words and actions and therefore express less
tolerant racial attitudes. In addition, there are several possibilities that combine various shadings of the
above two.

The same may also be said about party affiliation.
It has been found that party affiliation is a rather
durable and consistent factor in American political history. However, it has also been noted that in periods
immediately following landslide presidential victories,
there is a tendency for voters to identify with the party
of the victor.[22] Therefore, the same analysis that was
used in reference to attitudes may also be used here.
The professed party affiliation of the respondent may
well have influenced his electoral choice. By the same
token, however, the subject may have chosen the party
merely because of the great triumph of its standard
bearer. Here too, there are several intermediary possibilities which combine these two more absolute ones.

Nevertheless, while the relationship between party
affiliation and the vote may be somewhat ambiguous, it is
less so than the relationship between racial attitude and
the vote. This is because, given the great electoral

defeat Nixon inflicted upon McGovern, it might have been expected--were the vote to influence the subject's choice of party--that far more respondents would indicate that they were Republicans. The fact that the majority of respondents replied that they were Democrats and that many indicated that they had chosen the Democratic candidate in the other races seems to imply that the Nixon victory did not severely affect the partisan affiliations of many voters. At the very least, it can be said that the majority of respondents who indicated that they were Democrats represents a lower limit of Democrats and a large group for whom the Republican landslide had little impact upon their partisan affiliation. This distinction between association and causality and the qualifications it implies, however, must be borne in mind when analyzing the data being presented.

The discussion so far has proceeded in a rather simplistic vein. It has been implicitly assumed that the relationships studied in this chapter have been direct and viable. The data presented for religion have been analyzed independently from the data presented for party affiliation, which in turn have been analyzed independently from the data regarding racial attitude. It may be, however, that these variables are all involved in the voter's electoral habits. It has often been found that the vote is very much a result of either a "causal path" or a "funnel of causality" in which are involved numerous socioeconomic, attitudinal, psychological, and political factors.[23]

In addition, it is quite possible that each of the three variables found significant in the present study also relate significantly among themselves. In developing a model of the importance of religion in suburban voting, it would seem relevant to determine whether religion is significant in relation to party affiliation and racial attitude, the two most important variables in this study of suburban voting. If the three do relate significantly among themselves, then their respective relationships with the vote must be seen as a more mutual enterprise. If one or another does not relate significantly among the three, then perhaps an independent variable injected from a different direction or source may have been found.

Also, the data so far presented are rather coarse in the sense that they take into account only one independent and one dependent variable. The possibility of spuriousness has not been dealt with. It may well be that the relationship between religion and the vote will disappear when party affiliation is controlled. Should this occur, it might imply that the entire relationship between religion and the vote was only superficial and does not hold under controlled circumstances. Similarly, such a finding may imply that a relationship between religion and the vote does exist, but that the relationship is an indirect one in which party affiliation intervenes. It can readily be seen that controlled testing, in which each variable will be related to the vote while another is held constant, must be done before any meaningful inferences can be made.

Finally, it has been so far assumed that the significance of each variable is unidirectional: moving from some recess in the voter's field of perceptions or experiences toward the vote. It may be, however, that some of the relationships are multidirectional. They may move not only toward the vote but also toward another of the variables. For example, it may well be that though both party affiliation and racial attitude relate significantly to the vote, neither preceded the other in the causal model. Rather, party affiliation affects both the vote and the respondent's racial attitude, while the respondent's racial attitude affects both his vote and his party affiliation. The impact of either or both of the variables will then have been found to be toward the vote as well as toward the other variable. In addition, both variables may be found to move toward each other.

Despite these qualifications, however, one "common sense" assumption does seem warranted. It is reasonable that though there may be movement within religious groups --that is, from denomination to denomination--for socio-economic reasons, a respondent's religious identification is probably not caused by either his racial attitude or his partisan affiliation. Other possible relationships, however, remain to be tested.

Numerous questions have been raised regarding the nature, strength, and direction of causal inferences which can be made from the data presented in this chapter. Schematically, the possibilities may be shown as a causal path leading to the vote. Such a model is presented in Figure 3.2 below.[24]

Before detailing the diagram, three assumptions must be made explicit. The diagram takes into consideration only those variables found most significant in this chapter. Undoubtedly, other variables studied here or elsewhere also play some role. Also, the diagram assumes that some significant relationship exists between these three variables, an assumption that has yet to be proven. It is possible that some or all the variables act independently of the others and are not part of a coordinated causal path at all. In such a case, other models will have to be generated. Thirdly, the model assumes that even if a superficial relationship is found to disappear when controls are employed, the relationships are not spurious but merely direct. For example, if it should be found that the relationship between religion and the vote is zero when party affiliation is held constant, it may be that the original relationship was spurious. The diagram assumes, however, that the relationship between religion and the vote is not spurious but merely an indirect one in which party affiliation intercedes.

FIGURE 3.2

Schematic Model of the Possible Relationship of Variables Leading to the Ramapo Vote for 1972

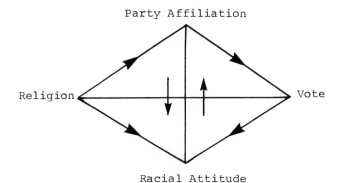

Party Affiliation

Religion

Vote

Racial Attitude

If one is prepared to bear in mind these three not unreasonable qualifications, the diagram may be employed. As indicated, religion may have a direct impact upon the vote. It is also possible that religion affects party affiliation, which in turn may have a direct impact on the vote. Alternatively, party affiliation may affect the voter's racial attitude which finally affects the vote.

The path may also move through racial attitude. Here, religion affects racial attitude, which may either directly affect the vote or which may affect party affiliation,

45

which will have a direct impact upon the vote. In addition, it should be noted that causal arrows have been
drawn in both directions between party affiliation and
racial attitude. This implies that no matter whether the
causal path moves from religion to racial attitude or to
party affiliation, the latter two variables may have a
mutual impact upon each other before either or both affect
the vote.

Finally, the diagram opens one more possibility. It
should not be construed that a causal model must move in
only one direction. The possible relationships being
analyzed are not "either-or" propositions. That is to
say that if religion is found to have a direct impact upon
the vote, it may also affect racial attitude. This may
have a direct impact upon the vote, as well as upon party
affiliation. Therefore, all the possibilities presented
may be true accounts of the causal path and may occur
simultaneously and in combination. This schematic analysis is not meant to be either exclusive or conclusive.
Rather, it is an outline of the manifold possibilities
which may be found to surface from the data detailed in
this chapter.

NOTES

    1. Wm. Dobriner, The Suburban Community (New York:
Putnam, 1958); V. O. Key, American State Politics (New
York: Knopf, 1956).
    2. S. Lubell, The Future of American Politics (New
York: Harper & Bros., 1952).
    3. See, for example, E. Banfield and J. Wilson,
City Politics (Cambridge: Harvard and M.I.T., 1963);
F. Wirt, "The Political Sociology of American Suburbia:
A Reinterpretation," Journal of Politics (August 1965):
647-66; J. Zikmund, "Comparison of Political Attitudes
and Activity Patterns in Central Cities and Suburbs,"
Public Opinion Quarterly (Spring 1967): 69-75.
    4. R. Dahl, Who Governs (New Haven: Yale, 1961).
    5. See, for example, G. Lenski, The Religious Factor
(Garden City: Doubleday, 1961); S. Carlos, "Religious
Participation and the Urban-Suburban Continuum," American
Journal of Sociology (March 1970): 742-59.
    6. See R. Wolfinger, "The Development and Persis-
tence of Ethnic Voting," American Political Science Re-
view (December 1965): 896-908; also M. Parenti, "Ethnic
Politics and the Persistence of Ethnic Identification,"
American Political Science Review (December 1967): 717-26.

7. See E. Banfield and J. Wilson, "Public Regardedness as a Value-Premise in Voting Behavior," American Political Science Review (September 1964): 876-87; see also their "Political Ethos Revisited," American Political Science Review (December 1971): 1048-62; also, M. Levey and M. Kramer, The Ethnic Factor (New York: Simon & Schuster, 1972).

8. G. Pomper, "Ethnic and Group Voting in Non-Partisan and Municipal Elections," Public Opinion Quarterly (Spring 1966): 79-97; also R. Lorinskas and B. Hawkins, "The Persistence of Ethnic Voting in Urban and Rural Areas," Social Science Quarterly (March 1969): 891-99.

9. S. Lieberson, "The Suburbs and Ethnic Residential Patterns," American Journal of Sociology (May 1962): 673-82.

10. See Parenti, op. cit.

11. Wirt, op. cit.

12. Lubell, op. cit., see chap. 4.

13. Lenski, op. cit.; also Carlos, op. cit.

14. See Levey and Kramer, op. cit., chap. 5, especially pp. 138-39; also L. Fuchs, John F. Kennedy and American Catholicism (New York: Meredith Press, 1967), especially pp. 116-21; also A. Greely, Why Can't They Be Like Us (New York: E. P. Dutton, 1971); also R. Merton, "The Latent Functions of the Machine," in E. Banfield, ed., Urban Government (New York: The Free Press, 1969), pp. 223-36.

15. This inference is supported by the insignificant nature of the difference between the Irish and all other Catholics in these two elections. In the presidential race, the data yielded: $x^2 = 1.03$ NS 1df, while for the congressional election the results were: $x^2 = .17$ NS 1df.

16. Key, op. cit., and Lubell, op. cit.

17. Berger, op. cit.

18. The terms belong to Robert Wood. See R. Wood, Suburbia: Its People and Their Politics (Boston: Houghton Mifflin, 1959), especially pp. 153-58.

19. F. Wirt et al., On the City's Rim (Lexington: D. C. Heath, 1972), see chap. 8; also, A. Campbell, White Attitudes Toward Black People (Ann Arbor: University of Michigan, 1971), see chap. 6.

20. Campbell, White Attitudes Toward Black People, op. cit., p. 120; O. Williams et al., Suburban Differences and Metropolitan Policies (Philadelphia: University of Pennsylvania, 1965), pp. 211-38; Wirt et al., On the City's Rim, op. cit., pp. 112-13.

21. Much of this discussion was suggested by the author's undergraduate instructor, Dr. Charles S. Liebman, presently chairman of the political science department at Bar-Ilan University, Ramat Gan, Israel. See also M. K. Jennings and H. Zeigler, "The Salience of American State Politics," American Political Science Review (June 1970): 523-35.

22. A. Campbell et al., The American Voter (New York: J. Wiley, 1960), chaps. 6 and 7; P. Converse, "The Concept of a Normal Vote," in A. Campbell et al., Elections and the Political Order (New York: J. Wiley, 1966), pp. 9-39; W. Flanagan, Political Behavior of the American Electorate (Boston: Allyn and Bacon, 1968), pp. 33-38. See also Survey Research Center data regarding partisan identification of voters, cited in Carr et al., Essentials of American Democracy (New York: Holt, Rinehart & Winston, 1968), p. 177.

23. Campbell et al., The American Voter, op. cit., chap. 2; also W. Miller and D. Stokes, "Constituency Influence in Congress," in Campbell et al., Elections and the Political Order, op. cit., pp. 351-72; also A. Goldberg, "Discerning a Causal Pattern Among Data on Voting Behavior," in H. M. Blalock, ed., Causal Models in the Social Sciences (Chicago: Aldine-Atherton, 1971), pp. 33-48.

24. The pattern for this model has been borrowed from Miller and Stokes, in Campbell et al., Elections and the Political Order, op. cit., p. 361.

4

POLITICAL
ATTITUDES

In the previous chapter, the relationship between ethnicity and the vote was analyzed. It was demonstrated that ethnicity as a variable was salient only when defined as religion. When Catholic respondents were further tested by nationality group, no consistently significant relationships surfaced. In addition, religion was significant only insofar as members of the same religious group tended to vote alike. However, the presence of a fellow-ethnic on the ballot, whether he was a Democratic or Republican candidate, had little effect on the voting habits of the various ethnic groups.

It was also found that religion was not the most important variable in the suburban vote. Judging by the magnitude of the contingency coefficient (C), two other variables had stronger relationships with the vote at all electoral levels: party affiliation and the respondent's attitude regarding residential segregation. Party affiliation was found to be far and away the most important variable in both national and local elections, while racial attitude was next. It was suggested that the actual vote is the result of a complex blending of these three variables (as well as other less important ones, to be sure), which may follow any (or many) of several causal paths.

Based upon these results, a number of suggestive questions and possibilities were raised in reference to the form and nature of such a causal path. It was conjectured that these three variables may be interrelated or independent of each other; they may operate in a singular or combined manner; they may move only toward the vote or toward each other as well; and they may be direct, indirect, or indeed only spurious and undetectable under controlled conditions.

This chapter deals with the issue of political attitudes and determines the importance of ethnicity in this area. Naturally, though a series of attitudes were tested in the present study, special attention will be paid to the importance of ethnicity and party affiliation in relation to racial attitude. This is because of the strong relationship found between racial attitude and the vote. Nevertheless, other attitudes are also important elements in the voter's field of political perceptions, and they merit study as well. Further, it must be recalled that even though the respondent's attitudes regarding residential segregation were found to be most important in voting, this does not mean that other attitudes were not important to him. It may only mean that he had little opportunity to act upon these attitudes given the nature of the candidates, the political environment in 1972, or the local political structure. Issues and attitudes only have electoral meaning if the voter has the opportunities and choices to act upon them. It is therefore deemed important to study several attitudes for what they may tell us about the present election as well as the potentials for future elections.[1]

AN OVERVIEW

Prior to presenting the present data, it would be useful to review briefly the existing literature regarding political attitudes, suburbia, and ethnicity, then set it to the context of the present study. As will be seen, much work has been done in the area of suburban political attitudes. Studies exist of the importance of ethnicity in the development of political attitudes, as well as the political attitudes of various ethnic groups. Little has been done, however, to link the two; that is, to study the importance of ethnicity in the suburbs, or the persistence of political attitudes ascribed to ethnic groups in the suburbs.

Major studies of political attitudes have yielded two conflicting schools of thought. One claims that social groups are the repositories of political attitudes and the individual takes his cues from the groups to which he belongs. A modification of this argument, though somewhat less socially deterministic, indicates that some 90 percent of the electorate cannot express a

50

meaningful political ideology and have little systematic understanding of electoral politics.[2] The second school of thought credits the citizen with far more interest and sophistication in the area of public affairs and claims that the voter is not only able to formulate opinions and attitudes on his own but, when a meaningful choice is offered to him he will vote consistently with his attitudes and opinions.[3]

Many analysts of suburban politics and society have opted for the first of the above schools when attempting to define and study suburban political attitudes. They reasoned that since most suburbs were homogeneous and most suburbanites (consciously or unconsciously) conformists, it is natural to assume that suburban voters would think, reason, and act alike.[4]

This like-mindedness and conformity was in turn attributed to one of two factors, analogous to the transplantation-conversion controversy outlined in Chapter 3. Some argued that suburbia was homogeneous because people with similar attitudes and values tend to seek each other out and reside near each other. This is the thrust of the transplantation argument.[5] It was alternatively hypothesized that suburbanites were conformers and "other-directed" because the nature of the suburbs demands similarity and consistency in the name of "community" and "social standards." This is quite similar to the conversion theory.[6] Rarely was the essential assumption of suburban homogeneity put to empirical test, however. It was just believed.

More recent studies have tested the assumption of suburban homogeneity and found it lacking. Considerable diversity has been found to exist socially, politically, and attitudinally from suburb to suburb. Further, socioeconomic and political diversities have also been found to exist within the same suburb.[7] It has also been noted that suburbs are often more different from each other than from their central cities.[8] Such findings have led some analysts to question the existence of a "suburban" set of attitudes or values.[9]

With few exceptions, ethnicity has not been seriously considered as an important variable in the area of suburban political values. Nevertheless, more general studies have indicated significant differences in the political attitudes of various ethnic and religious groups. It has been found, for example, that Jews tend to be more tolerant in the area of race relations and federal involvement in social affairs than non-Jews. Polish Catholics have

been found to be least tolerant in these areas.[10] Further,
ethnicity has proven to be a significant variable in the determination of the degree of a group's "public-regardedness";
that is, its willingness to support policies and programs
that do not serve its own immediate sectarian or parochial
needs.[11]

Though ethnicity has not been dealt with in terms of
suburban political attitudes, there is reason to believe
that it is significantly related to them. Much of the analysis outlined in the previous chapter relating to voting
habits may also be operative here. Though the conversion-
transplantation controversy--transposed in the context of
political attitudes to explain an assumed homogeneity--may
have been proven erroneous, some part of its logic may be
salvaged to support the present discussion. While suburbanites may be more diverse than assumed, it has nevertheless been found that the suburbs do engender a sense of
"community, identity and integration" among their residents, which encourages membership and participation in
religious and church-related groups.[12] It is no accident,
therefore, that participation and attendance in religious
activities is high in the suburbs.[13] The suburban resident may not be converted, but the more subtle forces en-
couraging him to participate in ethnoreligious activities
may well bring him closer to his fellow group members
either consciously or unconsciously.

If the suburban resident is "transplanting" his political attitudes, much the same may be argued. The finding
that considerable heterogeneity exists in the suburbs need
not contradict the theory that like-minded people seek
each other out. It need only modify the theory to exclude
the argument that all suburbs or even all of one suburb
will be "like-minded." Pockets of ethnic or religious
residential segregation may still exist, and indeed such
has been found to be the case.[14] Even in the suburbs, as
one author put it, ". . . a good Catholic can live most of
his life . . . within a Catholic environment . . . of
schools, religious endogamy, family, church, and social,
athletic, and youth organizations."[15]

It is most likely that the suburbanite is both converted and transplanted, albeit far less than earlier
theorists expected and assumed. He is probably somewhat
affected by his environs and no doubt brings prior sociopolitical attitudes and characteristics with him. To the
extent that he chooses suburbs--or communities within
suburbs--in which reside those like him, and he is subtly
encouraged to participate in the activities of these

communities, he will have been affected by both conversion and transplantation. If ethnoreligious identity is a part of the social structure of these communities--and the studies above suggest that it is--then ethnicity may be expected to be significantly related to the sociopolitical attitudes of suburban residents.

Thus far, the analysis has proceeded under the assumption that there is something peculiarly "suburban" in the attitudes of suburban residents. It has been found, however, that suburbs may often be more similar to their central cities than to other suburbs in measures of political attitudes.[16] Therefore, to discuss the role of ethnicity in suburban political attitudes may be an exercise in futility. Yet, assuming that the suburban resident is not significantly different than his nonsuburban analogue in the area of political attitudes, should it not also be expected, then, that ethnicity will be as important to him as it has been demonstrated to be generally? If it is true that Jews are more favorable to certain social policies, or Catholics different from non-Catholics on tests of "public-regardedness," should not these results be expected in suburban studies? Certainly these questions merit empirical analysis. The lack of such research may well be explained by the general disinterest of students of suburban politics in the effects of ethnicity there. Perhaps they have been so involved in explaining unproven hypotheses--for example, suburban Republicanism or homogeneity--or disproving them that they have made yet one more unproven assumption in their omission: that ethnicity plays little role in suburban politics.

On the basis of this cursory review and analysis of the existing literature, it is not unreasonable to assume that a significant relationship between ethnicity and political attitudes may exist. It must be conceded that the possible linkage between what has been said about suburban political attitudes and what has been said about the role of ethnicity in attitude formation merit study.

By and large, several propositions emerge from this analysis. It is first likely that strong and definitive relationships will surface between ethnicity--defined as religion generally and as nationality for Catholics additionally--and the respondents' attitudes toward certain issue-areas. Thus it is expected that voters of similar ethnic identification will think alike and therefore respond similarly.

Aside from testing the relationship between ethnicity and political attitudes independently, comparative analysis

will also be performed. Thus it may also be expected that
the relationship between ethnicity will be stronger and
more consistent than relationships to be found between
political attitudes and other variables of political, social, or demographic nature.

In order to lend scientific rigor and objectivity to
the analysis, these propositions have been organized into
formal hypotheses which allow more direct analysis. They
are outlined below:

1. On tests of general policy orientations, there
will be a greater correlation between political attitudes
and ethnicity than between political attitudes and any
other single variable.

- People of similar ethnic identity tend to
  view general policy areas similarly.
- Ethnicity will be more important than party
  identification, social class, issue interest,
  or candidate preference.

In order to test this hypothesis, subjects were asked
to respond to a series of statements regarding important
issues in local affairs. (These issue-areas were chosen
with the help of Republican and Democratic county leaders.)
The issues were: law and order, racial integration, drug
abuse, educational spending, welfare, the building of
high-rise apartment complexes, and trust in local government. Although all of the statements were couched in
local terms, it is recognized that some have more than
purely local implications, while others did not. One's
attitude toward the issue of law and order may well extend
beyond the immediate environs, while one's feelings about
high-rise apartments may be more parochial. The issues
have therefore been divided into two categories. The
first includes the more local areas: educational spending, the development of high-rise apartment buildings,
and trust in local government. The category of broader
concern includes: law and order, drug abuse, welfare,
and racial integration. The categories are intended for
the sake of convenience only, no exclusivity is implied.
It is recognized that they are somewhat arbitrary and
overlap at certain points.

THE LOCAL ISSUES

The first of the local issues to be studied is educational spending. If what has been written about ethnics
generally holds true, then it is expected that significant

differences would appear between the various groups in this area. Jews, especially, were expected to be significantly more favorable toward educational spending, as has been elsewhere argued.[17] As the following table indicates, no significant differences surfaced. (Although the questionnaire permitted respondents to "Agree Strongly" and "Disagree Strongly," it was necessary to collapse these categories to eliminate zeroes and facilitate the use of the chi-square statistic.)

Relationship between religion and support for educational spending. Statement: "Too much money is spent on public schools in this area."

Religion	Agree	No Opinion	Disagree
Prot. (n = 87)	34.5%	10.3%	55.2%
Cath. (n = 165)	37.0	14.5	48.5
Jew. (n = 206)	40.8	8.7	50.5

x^2 = 4.08 NS 4df

As the table shows, no significant differences exist between the groups in this area. In fact, what slight differences do exist run counter to expectations. Thus, Jews are somewhat more likely to agree with the statement; that is, Jews are less likely to support the educational spending level than the other two groups. The smaller group of Jewish respondents who indicated that they had no opinion in this area may further imply the greater importance of this area to Jews, although any such inference is mere speculation.

Much the same was the case when national background was tested against support of educational spending among Catholics. As the following indicates, no significant relationship surfaces.

Relationship between nationality, for Catholics, and support for educational spending. Statement: "Too much money is spent on public schools in this area."

Nationality	Agree	No Opinion	Disagree
Irish (n = 35)	37.1%	8.6%	54.3%
Italian (n = 74)	35.1	12.2	52.7
German (n = 24)	33.3	8.3	58.3

x^2 = .6 NS 4df

As is evident, all the nationality groups are virtually equal in their general support of educational spending in the local area, though German Catholics are somewhat more supportive. In this major local issue-area, no significant relationship has been found with ethnicity defined as either religion or nationality for Catholics.

Indeed, the strongest relationship to be found in this area is with occupation, a general pattern which will hold true for many of the attitudes under discussion. The following table shows this.

Relationship between occupation and educational spending. Statement: "Too much money is spent on public schools in this area."

Occupation	Agree	No Opinion	Disagree
Prof. (n = 117)	31.6%	6.0%	62.4%
Wh. Collar (n = 184)	39.1	9.2	51.6
Sk. Labor (n = 116)	43.1	12.1	44.8
Unskld (n = 70)	30.0	21.4	48.6

$$x^2 = 17.29 \qquad P = .01 \qquad C = .1852$$

As the data indicate, there is a generally positive relationship between support for educational spending and occupation; that is, the higher the status level of the respondent's occupation, the more likely is the respondent to support the level of educational spending. The exception to this general trend is the unskilled laborer. This category of respondents showed fairly strong support of educational spending locally. A number of possible explanations may exist for this discordant tendency. In the first instance, it has been elsewhere noted that those in the lowest socioeconomic class often support expensive public programs. This is done with the understanding that because of their lower income levels, and the progressive-graduated nature of the tax structure, they will not have to pay much of the cost.[18] Thus it is quite natural and rational for those at the lowest socioeconomic level to support the educational institution, no matter the cost.

Alternatively, it may be argued that the lowest class has accepted much of the "educational mystique" in the United States and sincerely believes that the way to increase one's station is through a better education. Therefore, no price is too high to pay for good schools and the improved living conditions that follow.

Finally, attention must be called to the "No Opinion" category. If this is taken into account, a different picture emerges. It will be noted that there is also a positive relationship between occupational status and opinion held; that is, the higher the level of occupational status, the more likely is the respondent to have an opinion regarding educational spending. The unskilled category has a large (21.4 percent) group of respondents who have admitted to no opinion; they thus imply either their lack of expertise or interest in this area, and/or its lack of importance to them. The findings may indeed be consistent with the positive trend but for the lowest class, whose responses are inconsistent because of the large group which has refused to indicate an opinion.

Another area of local concern which has been studied is the feeling of local residents regarding the development of high-rise apartment complexes in their area. This issue-area has implications in esthetic, environmental, and social terms. Again, it was found that no significant relationship exists between ethnicity and this attitude. The following table presents these data.

Relationship between religion and attitude toward the building of high-rise apartments. Statement: "I don't mind if high-rise apartments are built in this area."

Religion	Agree	No Opinion	Disagree
Prot. (n = 91)	12.1%	4.4%	83.5%
Cath. (n = 166)	13.9	10.8	75.3
Jew. (n = 207)	14.0	4.3	81.6

x^2 = 7.55 NS 4df

Quite clearly, the overwhelming majority of each group is opposed to the development of high-rise complexes in their area. Indeed, the general agreement in this area is in stark contrast with the earlier results regarding educational spending, in which considerable diversity was found. This general opposition to high-rise apartments may be credited to the urban encroachment it represents, as well as the increases in noise, traffic, and social problems which might be associated with it by respondents. As the table below indicates, no significant relationship was found to exist when nationality (for Catholics) was related with this issue-area.

Relationship between nationality, for Catholics, and the building of high-rise apartments. Statement: "I don't mind if high-rise apartments are built in this area."

Nationality	Agree	No Opinion	Disagree
Irish (n = 35)	20.0%	11.4%	68.6%
Italian (n = 73)	5.5	11.0	83.6
German (n = 25)	24.0	8.0	68.0

x^2 = 8.00 NS 4df

As the table indicates, no significant relationship has surfaced. Nevertheless, considerable difference of opinion seems to exist between Italians and other Catholics in this area. Though each group is strongly opposed to the development of high-rise apartments in their area, Italians seem far more so. This apparent difference bears closer scrutiny. The relationship between nationality and this attitude when Italians are compared to other Catholics is given below.

Relationship between Italian nationality, for Catholics, and attitude regarding high-rise apartment buildings.

Nationality	Agree	No Opinion	Disagree
Italian (n = 73)	5.5%	11.0%	83.6%
Other Cath. (n = 60)	21.7	10.0	68.3

$x^2 = 7.89$ P = .025 1df   C = .2366

As the table above shows, the difference between Italians and other Catholics is significant. This finding should not be considered unexpected. It has been noted that Italian Catholics are often characterized by an unusually strong attachment to their communities' neighborhoods. This attachment results in a negative reaction to impersonality and "bigness," and an attempt to carve out a comfortable and neighborly existence even in large urban centers.[19] The strong opposition to large apartment complexes may well be a manifestation of this community-neighborhood orientation; that is, the feeling that such high-rise apartments would not be in consonance with a "comfortable" life-style.

The data may also be interpreted differently. The reader will remember that the Italian respondents were actually not much different from Jewish and Catholic respondents. Of the Catholic respondents, 83.6 percent were opposed to high-rise developments, while the corresponding figures for Protestants and Jews were 83.5 percent and 81.6 percent respectively. It may be that Italians are not unusual in their opposition, but that German and Irish Catholics are unusually favorable to high-rise development. This possibility also bears further study. The following table presents the data for German and Irish Catholics compared to all others.

Relationship between Irish and German nationality, for Catholics, and attitude regarding high-rise apartment buildings. Statement: "I don't mind if high-rise apartments are built in this area."

Nationality	Agree	No Opinion	Disagree
German-Irish (n = 60)	21.7%	10.0%	63.3%
Others (n = 371)	11.5	5.7	82.5

$x^2 = 6.59$ P = .05 1df   C = .1228

As the table indicates, the differences between German and Irish Catholics and all other respondents are indeed significant in this attitude-area. Apparently, German and Irish respondents, though overwhelmingly opposed to the development of high-rise apartment complexes, are significantly less so than are all other respondents. Any attempts at explaining this phenomenon would be mere conjecture. The data would serve a local politician well, however. Apparently any local administration seeking to choose sites for such apartments should consider those areas in which reside German and Irish Catholics (if such concentrated areas exist) as the points of least opposition. The result, though not vital to the present study, does demand future analysis.

Though a significant difference surfaced between Italian subjects and other Catholics in the area of high-rise apartments, and the relationship bore a coefficient of C = .2366, this cannot be considered immediately relevant to the present hypothesis. The relationship surfaced only as a partial and peripheral result of the gross insignificance of the data regarding nationality in this attitude-area. It will be remembered that for all three Catholic nationality groups, no significant relationships appeared when compared by attitude regarding high-rise development (see the second table on page 57). Comparison between the former finding (regarding Italians as compared to all other Catholics) and those resulting from the correlation of other variables and this attitude would therefore be unfair. Nevertheless, this interesting "side" result of the data will be borne in mind for future reference.

Two related variables were actually the most significant when related to this attitude. These were occupation level and education. The following presents the relationship between occupation and the respondent's attitude in this area.

Relationship between occupation and attitude regarding high-rise apartment buildings. Statement: "I don't mind if high-rise apartments are built in this area."

Occupation	Agree	No Opinion	Disagree
Prof. (n = 118)	11.9%	3.4%	84.7%
Wh. Col. (n = 184)	15.2	5.4	79.3
Sk. Labor (n = 105)	11.4	9.5	79.0
Unskld (n = 76)	19.7	14.5	65.8

$$x^2 = 14.34 \quad P = .05 \ 6df \quad C = .1715$$

As the data indicate, there is, not unexpectedly, a negative relationship between occupation and favorability toward high-rise apartments. Those at the highest occupational level are most opposed to such developments, while those at the lowest level are most favorable, though all are largely opposed. A slight ambiguity, however, exists between the white collar and skilled labor groups; both are about equally opposed to high-rise building complexes. This relationship generally confirms the study of Williams et al., in Philadelphia. Their findings indicated that higher status suburbs were more likely to opt for higher taxes if lowering them meant large apartment and office buildings, while lower status suburbs were not likely to make the same choice.[20]

These findings, however, are not entirely confirmed by the data relating to education. The following presents this.

Relationship between education and the attitude toward the building of high-rise apartments. Statement: "I don't mind if high-rise apartments are built in this area."

Education Level	Agree	No Opinion	Disagree
Non-H.S. (n = 38)	10.5%	5.7%	84.2%
H.S. Grad. (n = 167)	15.6	10.8	73.7
Some College (n = 148)	17.6	4.7	77.7
Col. Grad. (n = 150)	11.3	6.0	82.7

$$x^2 = 17.16 \quad P = .01 \quad C = .1816$$

As the table indicates, there is no clearly defined relationship. Rather, the results are a study in ambiguity although, given those regarding occupation, it might have been expected that a similar negative relationship would exist. In fact, the data show that those with the lowest educational level are most opposed to the building of high-rise apartments, while those with some college were most likely to express a favorable opinion.

The data may be explained by the fact that in Ramapo many of those whose occupations are high status may not

have a strong education. This is particularly true in
terms of many wealthy real estate developers, builders,
and landowners, whose occupation and status may be professional but who have not attended college. Thus the
ambiguity may result.
    The final attitudinal measure at the local level
deals with trust in local government. It was only in
this one area that any relationship existed with ethnicity
and here only in terms of nationality, for Catholics. The
data below present the findings.
    Relationship between religion and trust in local gov-
ernment. Statement: "In general, we can usually trust
local officials to do what is right."

Religion	Agree	No Opinion	Disagree
Prot. (n = 89)	50.6%	16.9%	32.6%
Cath. (n = 166)	47.0	13.3	39.8
Jew. (n = 206)	38.8	14.6	46.6

$x^2 = 6.08$ NS 4df

    As the table shows, Jewish respondents were somewhat
less likely to indicate a trusting attitude toward local
government, while Protestants were most trusting. Nevertheless, the findings do not suggest any weighty differences between groups. (While Jewish respondents may seem
significantly less trusting to the reader, computations
do not bear this out. When Jews were tested against all
others, the results were $x^2 = 4.68$ NS 2df.) This, however, was not the case within the Catholic community.
Here it was found that major differences do exist, especially between German Catholics and others. The following presents these data.
    Relationship between nationality and trust in local
government (for Catholics). Statement: "In general, we
can usually trust local officials to do what is right."

Nationality	Agree	No Opinion	Disagree
Irish (n = 34)	41.1%	11.8%	47.1%
Italian (n = 72)	50.0	8.3	41.7
German (n = 26)	65.4	23.1	11.5

$x^2 = 11.03$ P = .05   C = .2776

    Quite clearly, German Catholics are overwhelmingly
trustful of local officials, while Irish Catholics are
least trustful of local officials. Unfortunately, these
data must be taken at face value, because the small size

of the sample and the distributions of the responses make
spurious testing and controlled analysis unreliable. It
is noteworthy, however, that the above relationship is
the strongest found in the area of political trust. The
second strongest relationship exists between trust in
local government and education. The following table presents this.

Relationship between education and trust in local
government. Statement: "In general, we can usually trust
local officials to do what is right."

Education Level	Agree	No Opinion	Disagree
Some H.S. (n = 39)	59.0%	23.1%	17.9%
H.S. Grad. (n = 165)	43.6	9.1	47.3
Some Col. (n = 148)	42.6	16.2	41.2
Col. Grad. (n = 145)	37.2	14.5	48.3

$$x^2 = 15.07 \qquad P = .025 \qquad C = .1715$$

As the data indicate, there is a fairly negative relationship between education and trust in local government. Those with the least education are most likely to
trust local officials, either because they know less about
government activities, they care less (see large percentage of "No Opinion"), or they feel less qualified to pass
negative judgment. The converse of each of these reasons
may serve to explain the responses of those with the most
education. A slight ambiguity exists, however, between
those with some college education and those with only a
high school diploma. Once again, this may be somewhat
due to the ambiguity of occupational positions; that is,
some of those who have only graduated from high school
may well be earning more as real estate developers or
landowners than some of those with partial college education. On the whole, however, the negative relationship
is fairly constant.

These, then, have been the findings relevant to
local issues.

Ethnicity, both in terms of religion and in terms of
nationality, does not play a role in the areas of educational spending, the development of high-rise apartment
complexes, and political trust.

An exception to this is the relationship between
nationality and political trust for Catholics. It was
here found that German Catholics are significantly more
trusting of local officials than other Catholics.

The most important determinants of these local political attitudes are social class, defined in terms of
education and occupation.

It should be noted that these data further deny the myth of mass suburban conformity. Diversity exists both socially (different levels of education and occupation exist) and attitudinally. Not only are there "class" differences, but these differences translate themselves into attitudinal differences in at least three major local issues. Notable for their absence in this area are ethnicity and party affiliation. Yet it will be remembered that none of these issues played important roles in determining the voting preferences of the respondents (see Chapter 3). It may be that these issues were either not clearly defined by the candidates or not of great importance to the voter in his electoral decision. It remains yet to study the relationships in the more broad, social questions of drug abuse, law and order, racial integration, and welfare before further speculation can proceed.

THE BROADER ISSUES

In addition to those issues which have largely local implications, respondents' attitudes about broader social issues were also tested, albeit within the local context. In these areas, party affiliation and ethnicity did play a more significant role, although occupation and education were still found to be important.

The first such attitude to be analyzed deals with the issue of law and order, which has broad implications in terms of racial and urban tensions. As the following table shows, no relationship was found between religion and attitude on law and order.

Relationship between religion and attitude regarding law and order. Statement: "Local law enforcement officials have been unfairly handicapped in their attempts to prevent crime in this community."

Religion	Agree	No Opinion	Disagree
Prot. (n = 91)	41.8%	15.4%	42.9%
Cath. (n = 168)	44.6	14.3	41.1
Jew. (n = 207)	36.7	20.8	42.5

$x^2 = 4.04$ NS 4df

As the data indicate, no significant difference exists between the religious communities on the law and order issue. It can be noted that Catholics are somewhat more likely to feel that the law enforcement function is unfairly handicapped, while Jews are somewhat more ambivalent on this issue. Yet the differences are small. It is also notable that the community as a whole seems almost evenly split in this issue-area, one more sign of the diversity of opinion in this suburb.

Similarly, no significant relationship exists between nationality and attitude on law and order, for Catholic respondents. These data are presented below.

Relationship between nationality and attitude on law and order, for Catholic respondents. Statement: "Local law enforcement officials have been unfairly handicapped in their attempts to prevent crime in this community."

Nationality	Agree	No Opinion	Disagree
Irish (n = 35)	45.7%	17.1%	37.1%
Italian (n = 73)	49.3	13.7	37.0
German (n = 26)	38.5	11.5	50.0

x^2 = 1.42 NS 4df

Interestingly, although no strong relationships surfaced in this area, the two most significant variables were education and party affiliation. The importance of education continues the trend of significance of socio-economic status earlier noted. Party affiliation, however, was conspicuously absent as a variable in more purely local affairs.

The relationship between party affiliation and attitude regarding law and order is detailed below. Statement: "Local law enforcement officials have been unfairly handicapped in their attempts to prevent crime in this community."

Party	Agree	No Opinion	Disagree
Republican (n = 162)	48.8%	15.4%	35.8%
Democratic (n = 282)	35.8	16.7	47.5

x^2 = 7.61   P = .025   C = .1301

As the data show, there is a significant difference between Republicans and Democrats in this area. Apparently, Republicans seem more likely to agree that law enforcement officials are being unfairly handicapped, while Democrats are less likely to feel so. Thus, not only is there a diversity of partisan affiliation in this suburb but apparently, in this issue-area, the affiliation has some meaning in terms of attitudes. The relationship, however, is not a strong one (C = .1301) and is second in importance to education as a variable in this area. The following table presents these data.

Relationship between level of education and attitude on law and order. Statement: "Local law enforcement officials have been unfairly handicapped in their attempts to prevent crime in this community."

Education Level	Agree	No Opinion	Disagree
Some H.S. (n = 39)	46.2%	25.6%	28.2%
H.S. Grad. (n = 168)	44.0	14.9	41.1
Some Col. (n = 150)	40.0	19.3	40.6
Col. Grad. (n = 148)	34.5	14.2	51.4

$$x^2 = 14.2 \qquad P = .05 \; 6df \qquad C = .1653$$

As the table shows, there is a generally negative relationship between education and agreement that local law enforcement officials are being unfairly handicapped. Those with only some high school education are most likely to agree with the statement (46.2 percent), while college graduates are least likely to agree (34.5 percent). The fairly high percentage of "No Opinion" responses, especially among non-high school graduates, indicates a somewhat ambivalent feeling among the respondents which must also be considered in analyzing the data. Perhaps the law enforcement issue is not all that important to these suburban dwellers. Indeed, they may see this problem as a peculiarly urban one from which they have escaped. The even split of opinions on this issue, and the rather low value of C may serve to support this argument.

The second issue among these broader social issues regards drug abuse. In this area, a significant relationship with religious identification was found. The following table presents these data.

The relationship between religion and attitude regarding drug abuse. Statement: "Drug abuse is the major issue facing our town."

Religion	Agree	No Opinion	Disagree
Prot. (n = 87)	44.8%	25.3%	29.9%
Cath. (n = 166)	56.0	15.1	28.9
Jew. (n = 206)	47.1	11.7	41.3

$$x^2 = 14.15 \qquad P = .01 \qquad C = .1729$$

Though the data indicate a significant relationship, the results are difficult to interpret. The most notable finding relative to the Protestant respondents is the large group of "No Opinion" responses, possibly indicating their lack of interest or information in this area.

Catholics are apparently much more concerned with the
question of drug abuse, while Jews are less concerned.

Though religion was found to be significantly related to the respondents' attitude regarding drug abuse,
nationality--for Catholics--was not, as the table below
shows.

Relationship between nationality, for Catholics, and
attitude regarding drug abuse. Statement: "Drug abuse
is the major issue facing this town."

Nationality	Agree	No Opinion	Disagree
Irish (n = 34)	55.9%	8.8%	35.3%
Italian (n = 73)	54.8	11.0	34.2
German (n = 25)	52.0	16.0	32.0

x^2 = .75   NS 2df

As the table indicates, the differences between the
various Catholic nationality groups are not significant.
Apparently, the Irish are slightly more concerned about
drug abuse than any of the other groups, while the Germans are slightly less concerned. Given the close nature
of the responses in all categories, no meaningful inferences can be made.

The relationship with religion, however, is not the
strongest in the area of drug abuse, judging by the C
values (C = .1719). Once again, the strongest relationship is with the variable of education, further indicating the important role of variables involved with socioeconomic status in the determination of political attitudes. The table below shows this.

Relationship between education and attitude regarding drug abuse. Statement: "Drug abuse is the major
issue facing this town."

Education Level	Agree	No Opinion	Disagree
Some H.S. (n = 39)	33.3%	33.3%	23.1%
H.S. Grad. (n = 166)	16.9	16.9	26.5
Some Col. (n = 146)	13.0	13.0	35.6
Col. Grad. (n = 146)	11.6	11.6	44.5

x^2 = 22.02   P = .005 6df   C = .2059

Evidently, a significant relationship exists between
education and concern over drug abuse. College graduates
are unlikely to feel that drug abuse is the major issue
facing the town (43.8 percent), while those with a high
school education only seem most concerned (56.6 percent).

Somewhat difficult to interpret are the data regarding those with least education. These respondents registered the lowest percentage of both "Agree" and "Disagree" responses. Perhaps the key to inference here is their exceptionally high percentage of "No Opinion" responses (33.3 percent). These respondents seem either not interested in this area or consider themselves incompetent to pass judgment on this issue. Such a reading, however, is tentative and must await further study.

The next issue, one which has clearly national implications and was not really couched in local terms, deals with welfare. It was found that welfare attitudes did not correspond significantly with ethnicity. Rather, the issue is apparently a partisan one; that is, the most significant correlation was with party affiliation. The following table presents the data.

Relationship between religion and attitudes regarding welfare. Statement: "People on welfare get too much for nothing."

Religion	Agree	No Opinion	Disagree
Prot. (n = 91)	47.3%	14.3%	38.5%
Cath. (n = 164)	43.3	19.5	37.2
Jew. (n = 207)	40.1	17.4	42.5

x^2 = 2.4 NS 4df

As the above indicate, there is no significant relationship between religious identification and attitudes about welfare. It may be noted, however, that Jews are most tolerant toward welfare recipients and Protestants are least tolerant. When these attitudes are related with nationality among Catholic respondents, the results are similar--no significant relationship results. The following table presents these findings.

Relationship between nationality and attitude regarding welfare for Catholic respondents.

Nationality	Agree	No Opinion	Disagree
Irish (n = 35)	37.1%	20.0%	42.9%
Italian (n = 73)	49.3	23.3	27.4
German (n = 25)	28.0	20.0	52.0

x^2 = 7.78 NS 4df

Although the table indicates no significant differences between the various Catholic national communities, one is struck by the diversity of the responses. As was the case in the areas of political trust and law enforcement, German Catholics and Italian Catholics are most different. Italian respondents are least tolerant toward those on welfare and, judging from the large number of "No Opinion" responses, somewhat ambivalent toward the entire issue. German Catholics are most tolerant toward welfare recipients and somewhat less ambivalent about the welfare question. Apparently, the starkest differences within the Catholic community exist between Italians and Germans. The reader is cautioned, however, to keep in mind that the data are not significant. This was also the case when Italian and German respondents were compared directly; that is, the differences were not significant (x^2 = 5.36 NS 2df).

The most significant variable in the welfare issue-area was that of party affiliation, though it should be noted that the value of C is not extremely high. Data on this follow.

Relationship between party affiliation and attitude regarding welfare. Statement: "People on welfare get too much for nothing."

Party	Agree	No Opinion	Disagree
Republican (n = 160)	52.5%	19.4%	28.1%
Democratic (n = 280)	38.9	14.6	46.4

$$x^2 = 14.25 \qquad P = .005 \qquad C = .1772$$

As the table indicates, it seems that Republicans are apparently less tolerant of welfare recipients than are Democrats. Further, even among those Republicans who did not agree with the statement, a large percentage did not disagree. Thus, the difference between those Democrats who disagreed and those Republicans who disagreed is larger. Again, it is apparent that the party affiliation of the respondent does have some content in terms of political attitudes. It is also interesting that in this area, which has both social and economic overtones, neither of the chief socioeconomic variables--education and occupation--proved significant (x^2 = 9.97 6df and x^2 = 12.36 6df, respectively). It may be that as issues become broader and less purely local in scope, socioeconomic status recedes as a significant variable in favor of party affiliation. Therefore, in the areas of drug abuse and law enforcement, it is not unusual to find education playing an important role. Though these attitudes have been classified among the "broader" issues, they still have considerable local impact. In the much broader-based question of welfare, which may have more urban connotations, partisan factors become more significant.

This finding may have interesting implications. If broader issue-areas may be differentiated from those with largely local significance, then it may be that in the area of attitudes party affiliation has lost some of its impact. Though it has been found that attitudes are strongly related to partisan affiliation in national samples, this does not seem to hold for the present sample when local issues are tested. To this extent, the earlier hypothesis which postulated a weakening of the party tie at the local level has been partially confirmed. The further speculation that ethnicity would replace party affiliation as the major variable in relation to these attitudes has not been confirmed. Rather, socioeconomic class, measured in terms of occupation and education, has taken precedence.

It must be noted, however, that the categories created are somewhat arbitrary. It may be argued that the overlap between what has been considered local and what has been termed "broader" is too great to permit the categorization to be used as an explanatory tool. Without admitting to the strength of this criticism, a second explanation may be offered. Perhaps the cutting edge may lie in the area of electoral relevance--the degree to which a particular element is related to the respondent's voting habits in 1972.

The concept of an "electoral perspective" was briefly introduced in the past chapter in relation to the activity of the C statistic at the various electoral levels (see Chapter 3). It might be well to expand on this analysis. Prior theorists have postulated the existence of various theoretical models which help explain voting activity. An example of such a tool is Campbell's "funnel of causality" in which various electoral identifications, socioeconomic factors, and attitudes combine sequentially to determine the vote.[21] It may be that in addition there is a time-bound element which serves as the selective element in any given election. Thus, while it may be that over time certain factors prove to have consistent significance, only some of these will have significance in a given election. Further, the relative importance of even those variables that are regularly important will vary from election to election.

Therefore, it is not sufficient to conclude that "attitudes" or "party" are important variables. Which attitudes or the role of the party must also be considered as a varying element in the electoral decision. This time-bound element is here being termed the "electoral perspective"; that is, those variables which seem to be most clearly related to the vote. In the present data, the electoral perspective is primarily composed of the respondent's party affiliation, racial attitude, and religious identification.

It seems, then, that the attitudes most likely to relate strongly to these three variables are those which have the greatest impact upon the vote. As the data in the past chapter imply, such attitudinal variables as political trust and high-rise development were at no time related to the vote, while attitudes regarding law and order and welfare were significantly related--three and two times respectively. A most clear indication of this postulation would result if it can be indicated that the attitude most related electorally--that regarding residential integration--relates significantly to party affiliation and religion.

Two inferences may be made based upon this analysis. First, it may be expected that should any of the more local, non-electoral issues be given greater prominence in future elections then it may become part of the "electoral perspective" for that time and relate significantly with party affiliation or religion--assuming these remain in the "perspective." Second, it should be expected that racial attitude will relate significantly to each of the other two variables. The following table presents the data. This test will be analyzed shortly.

Relationship between religion and attitude toward residential integration. Statement: "I see nothing wrong with Black people moving onto this block."

Religion	Agree	No Opinion	Disagree
Prot. (n = 91)	30.8%	30.8%	38.5%
Cath. (n = 166)	31.9	30.7	37.3
Jew. (n = 205)	49.3	29.3	21.5

$$x^2 = 19.15 \quad P = .005 \quad C = .2003$$

As the table shows, the differences between Protestants and Catholics are not great. Both are about evenly divided on the issue, with a plurality being opposed to residential integration. Jews, however, are quite unlike both Protestant and Catholic respondents. Jews were far more tolerant in this issue, almost half favored residential integration, and less than a quarter were in opposition. Notable for all groups is the high number of "No Opinion" responses. It is unlikely that the race issue

is one in which they have no interest or information.
Rather, it may be one of such import and personal impact
that respondents were unwilling to discuss it with the
interviewer. Also, for present purposes, it is noteworthy
that religion does play an important and significant part
in the area of racial attitudes. As the following table
indicates, however, the same cannot be said about nationality differences within the Catholic community.

Relationship between nationality and attitude regarding residential integration, for Catholics. Statement:
"I see nothing wrong with Black people moving onto this
block."

Nationality	Agree	No Opinion	Disagree
Irish (n = 35)	37.1%	28.6%	34.3%
Italian (n = 71)	28.2	28.2	43.7
German (n = 26)	34.6	38.5	26.9

x^2 = 2.95 NS 4df

Clearly, no significant relationship emerges from
these data. Again, however, it should be noted that Italians and Germans are on opposite attitudinal extremes. A
large plurality of Italian respondents disagreed with the
statement (43.7 percent), whereas about one-fourth of the
German respondents disagreed (26.9 percent). The large
number of Germans who did not register an opinion (38.5
percent) is also noteworthy in comparison with Italians,
although the insignificant nature of the data makes further analysis dangerous.[22] Suffice it to say that the
data further suggest the previous findings regarding the
attitudinal differences between Italian and German Catholics.

A stronger relationship than that between religion
and racial attitude was found when party affiliation was
related to racial attitude. This suggests the interrela-
tionship between the three variables which were most important in relation to the vote. The following table presents the data.

Relationship between party affiliation and attitude
on residential integration. Statement: "I see nothing
wrong with Black people moving onto this block."

Party	Agree	No Opinion	Disagree
Republican (n = 160)	23.1%	31.3%	45.6%
Democratic (n = 273)	49.1	31.1	19.8

Quite clearly, the attitude regarding residential segregation is one on which local partisans divide. Apparently, Republicans are far less tolerant about residential integration than are Democrats. Over twice as many Democrats agree with the statement than Republicans, while more than twice as many Republicans than Democrats disagree. The large group of those who manifest no opinion among both parties is also of note.

It seems that these three variables which were found to be important in relation to the vote are also significant in relation to each other. It has been demonstrated that party affiliation and racial attitude are significantly related. It has also been demonstrated that religion and racial attitude are significantly related. This latter finding also confirms the previous studies of Wirt et al., and Campbell.[23]

One final link remains to be tested. Although both religion and party affiliation have been shown to be significantly related to racial attitude, they have not been tested against each other. In order to confirm the belief that none of the variables operates independently of each other in the causal procession toward the vote, it must also be demonstrated that a significant relationship between religion and party affiliation exists. Though party affiliation does not represent a political attitude in any pure sense, it is relevant to test this relationship now. As the following table indicates, a significant relationship does exist.

Relationship between religion and party affiliation.

Religion	Republicans	Democrats
Prot. (n = 78)	51.3%	48.7%
Cath. (n = 149)	46.3	53.7
Jew. (n = 178)	22.5	77.5

$$x^2 = 28.54 \quad P = .001 \quad 2 \text{ df} \quad C = .2566$$

As is clear from the data, significant differences exist between the various religious groups in terms of their partisan preferences. Most striking is the Jewish preference for the Democratic Party, while Protestants are the only group whose majority indicated a Republican preference.

Apparently, none of the three variables under discussion—party affiliation, religion, and racial attitude—operates independently from any of the others. All are related in the causation of the vote. The reader is again reminded that the statistical tests being employed indicate only association and not causation. While significant relationships have been found to exist, the direction of these relationships is not implied by the statistics.

SUBURBAN ATTITUDES: A SUMMARY

Briefly, the following has been found in relation to political attitudes in Ramapo, 1972-73. The most consistently significant variables in more purely local issues--educational spending, the building of high-rise apartments, and local political trust--were education and occupation. Apparently, class differences do exist in this suburb, and these differences translate themselves in terms of attitudes, especially in the local political arena. Contrary to the hypothesis, ethnicity by any definition was found to be of little significance in this attitude category. Also, contrary to findings presented in relation to the vote, party affiliation was not found to be significant in this local attitude area.

As the attitude areas under discussion broadened to include such issues as law and order, drug abuse, and welfare, partisanship and religion were found to be more significant. In explaining this result, it was suggested that the variables of religion, and especially partisan affiliation, may be important to the respondent only in an electoral setting, in which socioeconomic class apparrently had little importance. The broader issues may have been given greater coverage and emphasis by the candidates and therefore were related in the voter's mind to party affiliation and religious identification. This supposition was strengthened by the significant nature of the relationship between party affiliation and racial attitude--the most important attitude variable in relation to the vote and between religion and racial attitude.

This finding is also relevant in terms of the causal model introduced in the past chapter. It was they hypothesized that the three variables found to be strongly related to the vote--religion, party affiliation, and racial attitude--might also be related to each other. It was shown in this chapter that significant relationships do indeed exist between all three variables. This seems to eliminate one set of possibilities studied in the previous chapter: that all or some of these variables act independently from the others in relating to the vote.

It remains yet to compare and test these variables under controlled circumstances. Such analysis will permit some direction for the data to emerge. While it seems reasonable that religion is not caused by the other two variables, only this "common sense" can be applied. The direction, sequence, and combination of the variables beyond that is still open to question. A further analysis of the various possibilities will await a later chapter.

NOTES

1. For a further development of this point, see P. Bachrach and M. Baratz, "Two Faces of Power," American Political Science Review (December 1962): 947-52; also, R. Wolfinger, "Non-Decisions and the Study of Local Politics," American Political Science Review (December 1971): 1063-80.

2. B. Berelson et al., The People's Choice (New York: Columbia University, 1968), chap. 5; A. Campbell et al., The American Voter (New York: J. Wiley, 1960), chap. 9.

3. See V. O. Key, The Responsible Electorate (Cambridge: Harvard University, 1966); also G. Pomper, "From Confusion to Clarity: Issues and the American Voters, 1956-1968," American Political Science Review (June 1972): 415-28; also D. Repass, "Issue Salience and Party Choice," same journal (June 1971): 389-400; also B. Page and R. Brody, "Policy Voting and the Electoral Process," same journal (September 1972): 979-95; also G. Kramer, "Short-Term Fluctuations in U.S. Voting Behavior," same journal (March 1971): 131-43.

4. See R. Wood, Suburbia: Its People and Their Politics (Boston: Houghton-Mifflin, 1958), especially chap. 1; A. Spectorsky, The Exurbanites (Philadelphia: Lippincott, 1956).

5. R. Fairly, "Suburban Persistence," American Sociological Review (February 1964): 38-47; also F. Wirt, "The Political Sociology of American Suburbia: A Reinterpretation," The Journal of Politics (August 1965): 647-66.

6. W. Whyte, The Organization Man (New York: J. Wiley, 1956); D. Reisman, "The Suburban Dislocation," Annals of the American Academy of Political and Social Sciences (November 1957): 130-41.

7. B. Berger, Working-Class Suburb (Berkeley: University of California, 1960); W. Dobriner, Class in the Suburbs (Englewood Cliffs: Prentice-Hall, 1963); Wirt, op. cit.

74

8. J. Zikmund, "A Comparison of Political Attitudes and Activity Patterns in Central Cities and Suburbs," Public Opinion Quarterly (Spring 1967): 69-75; F. Wirt et al., On the City's Rim (Lexington: Heath and Co., 1972), especially chaps. 8 and 9; A. Campbell, White Attitudes Toward Black People (Ann Arbor: University of Michigan, 1971), especially chap. 6.

9. Ibid., see also S. Donaldson, The Suburban Myth (New York: Columbia University, 1969).

10. Campbell, White Attitudes Toward Black People, op. cit., chap 3; also A. Greely, Why Can't They Be Like Us (New York: Institute of Human Relations, 1969), see especially the table on p. 46.

11. E. Banfield and J. Wilson, "Public-Regardedness as a Value Premise in Voting Behavior," American Political Science Review (September 1964): 876-87; see also their "Political Ethos Revisited," same journal (December 1971): 1048-62.

12. S. Carlos, "Religious Participation and the Urban-Suburban Continuum," American Journal of Sociology (March 1970): 742-59.

13. Ibid., also G. Lenski, The Religious Factor (Garden City: Doubleday, 1961); also J. Kramer and S. Levantman, Children of the Gilded Ghetto (New Haven: Yale University, 1961).

14. S. Lubell, The Future of American Politics (New York: Harper & Bros., 1952), especially chap. 4; also S. Lieberson, "Suburbs and Ethnic Residential Patterns," American Journal of Sociology (May 1962): 673-81.

15. M. Parenti, "Ethnic Politics and the Persistence of Ethnic Identification," American Political Science Review (December 1967): 717-26.

16. Zikmund, op. cit.

17. See, for example, L. Fuchs, The Politics of the American Jews (Glencoe: The Free Press, 1956).

18. Banfield and Wilson, op. cit.

19. D. Moynihan and N. Glazer, Beyond the Melting Pot (Cambridge: Harvard University and M.I.T., 1970).

20. O. Williams et al., Suburban Differences and Metropolitan Politics (Philadelphia: University of Pennsylvania, 1965), especially pp. 211-38.

21. Campbell et al., The American Voter, op. cit., chap. 9.

22. Ibid., chap. 2; also W. Miller and D. Stokes, "Constituency Influence in Congress," in A. Campbell et al., Elections and the Public Order, op. cit., pp. 351-72; also A. Goldberg, "Discerning a Causal Pattern Among

Data on Voting Behavior," in H. M. Blalock, ed., <u>Causal Models in the Social Sciences</u> (Chicago: Aldine-Atherton, 1971), pp. 33-48.

23. Wirt et al., <u>On the City's Rim</u>, op. cit., pp. 115-25; also Campbell, <u>White Attitudes Toward Black People</u>, op. cit., pp. 119-25.

Another variable which has been tested in this analysis of the politics of suburbia is the degree and amount
of political interest and participation characteristic of
the respondents. This area was measured in terms of the
subject's exposure to the local media (local newspapers
and radio), as well as his avowed interest, voting, and
participation in local political discussions. Prior to
analyzing the resultant data, it would be well to outline
the major trends in the scholarly literature, relevant to
political interest and participation in the suburbs.

AN OVERVIEW

It has been noted generally that the most important
variables in determining the extent of a citizen's political involvement are political efficacy, strength of party
identification, and political trust.[1]

The subject of political participation in the suburbs
has produced contradictory strains in the literature. First
is the noninvolvement school which claims that the suburban resident is so busy commuting or "Kaffeeklatsch-ing"
that little time is left for political interest or involvement;[2] in contrast, the hyperinvolvement school
claims that enormous political activity exists for each
minute detail of governance and administration.[3]

Three reasons are given by the second group for the
frenetic level of political activity in the suburbs: (1)
The suburbanite is generally a homeowner (often for the
first time) and is thus concerned with assessments, sewer
taxes, and local school taxes which otherwise might be

left to the landlord;[4] (2) The suburban resident is not
as anonymous as he might have been in the city, and his
neighbors demand from him "some civic-mindedness which he
dare not altogether refuse";[5] and (3) The suburban resident lives in a homogeneous community which encourages
interaction and group participation.[6] Ironically, however,
even among those of the hyperinvolvement school, a general
feeling exists that though the level of political participation is high, the participation is generally meaningless,
trivial, and highly parochial.[7]

In addition, except to compare members of one religious group to another in the general area of political
interest, ethnic or religious identification has not been
seriously regarded as a major variable in the area of political participation, suburban or otherwise.[8]

Nevertheless, there may be some reason to believe
that ethnicity will be significantly related to political
participation. Much of what has been argued in earlier
chapters in regard to voting and attitudes may also apply
here. Apparently, ethnic enclaves exist in the suburbs
and suburbanites actively participate in religious activities. Since prior studies of suburban political interest
have attributed its characteristic "hyperinvolvement" to
largely community-neighborhood factors, it is not unreasonable to assume that communities that have ethnoreligious
bases will be so bent in their residential influences.

Further, there may well be some relationship between
the community-orientation which leads to this hyperactiv-
ity and ethnicity. Participation in suburban church activities may well be related to the cultural-communal
values that earlier authors have found. The same forces
which encourage the suburbanite to engage in--or at least
follow--local politics actively may be the ones which encourage him to participate in religious activities.

This analysis may also conform to those of the noninvolvement school. It is here argued that suburbanites
are too busy with a variety of social activities to participate politically. Perhaps part of that social involvement is based upon ethnic or religious activities
which have often been found to fulfill social as well as
spiritual needs. If this be the case, it may not be unreasonable to assume that the degree of political participation will vary by ethnoreligious group; that is, the
extent to which the group either fulfills the social needs
of the participant or encourages him to participate politically.

It is, of course, to be noted that the data included in prior chapters have not borne out the "ethnic" hypothesis. By and large, ethnicity has not proven to be of major importance in relation to either the suburban vote or the political attitudes of suburban voters. This need not negate the chance of its importance here, however.

Prior studies of political interest have indicated that it is positively related to strength of partisan affiliation. It has been demonstrated that the stronger the partisanship, the more likely is the respondent to indicate political interest. Assuming that this relationship holds true in the suburbs (and the tenacity of party affiliation demonstrated in the two previous chapters gives considerable indication that it might), it may be that those elements related to partisanship will also play a role in political interest levels. If this should be the case, then ethnicity may be quite important as such a variable.

While it may be true that ethnicity relates to voting and attitudes under very limited circumstances only, this may not be the case with interest. Interest levels are further detached from the immediate area of attitudes and the vote. When asking for an opinion, the interviewer already assumes that one exists. Perhaps attitudinal tests tap a psychological area that exists only superficially and is forced into existence only in response to the question. Therefore, the fact that most attitudes do not relate significantly to the respondent's ethnic identity may be a "spurious" finding predicated upon the assumption that the attitude actually plays a role in the respondent's political perceptions. Perhaps interest is a far better measure.

It should be remembered that though ethnicity did not generally relate to voting and political attitudes, religion did relate significantly to the vote--under certain limited circumstances--and to certain electorally relevant attitudes. In fact, it has been postulated (see chapter 4) that ethnicity may be considered part of the 1972 "electoral perspective." If this is true, then it is reasonable to expect that many of the tests of political interest which are quite clearly "electoral," such as voter turnout, attention to local news, and frequency of political discussions, will relate significantly to ethnicity.

It is now relevant to test the veracity of these assumptions empirically. Aside from detailing the above analyses, such a test of the influence of ethnicity upon political interest and participation in the suburbs would fill a presently existing gap in the political literature. Essentially, it is argued that ethnicity will be strongly related to the level of voter participation and interest in the suburbs. Such interest will be manifest in terms of the regularity of voter turnout, as well as the respondent's self-assessment of his political interest.

In addition, those elements which surround political interest and point to it will also be tested. Thus, the relationship between ethnicity and the regularity with which respondents listen to local news on the local radio station, or read about it in the local paper, may also be of importance. As such, ethnicity will be of greater importance in relation to these indexes of political interest and participation than other socioeconomic, demographic, and political variables under discussion.

To allow stricter and more cogent empirical analysis, these propositions have been reduced to straightforward hypotheses as follows:

1. There will be a greater relationship between ethnicity and interest in local politics than between ethnicity and any other variable.

   • Interest is defined in terms of nonvoting, the tendency to follow local politics on the local radio or in local newspapers, to discuss it with friends and relatives, and the self-assessment of the respondent.
   • A stronger relationship will be found between ethnicity and interest in local politics than between interest and class, party affiliation, issue-interest, or candidate perception.

As the language of these propositions implies, several measures of political interest-participation have been employed. These include certain variables which are more related to the respondent's attention to local affairs and the media, for example, the tendency to get information through the local newspaper or radio. In addition, certain of these are more direct measures of the respondent's actions or interest in the political arena: voting, self-assessed interest, and so forth. For this reason the following data has been divided between these two measures. The variables related to attention to local affairs will be discussed first. It is well that these measures of interest be related to ethnicity to determine if ethnicity is significant in this area.

ETHNICITY AND THE LOCAL MEDIA

In order to ascertain the degree of exposure of the respondents to the local media, subjects were asked to determine the frequency with which they read local newspapers and listened to the local radio. It might first be noted that the overwhelming number of respondents indicated that they read the local newspaper and listened to the local radio quite often. It is also of interest here to determine the significance of ethnicity in relation to these claims. The table below presents this.

Relationship between religion and frequency of local radio listening.

Religion	At Least Once/Week	Less Often	Never
Prot. (n = 88)	46.6%	18.2%	35.2%
Cath. (n = 163)	63.8	7.4	28.9
Jew. (n = 199)	61.8	9.5	28.6

$x^2 = 10.8$ P = .05 4df   C = .1530

As the data indicate, members of different religious groups do differ in the extent to which they listen to local radio. Catholics and Jews, in that order, are considerably more likely to gain information from the local radio station than are Protestants. Further, among those who do listen, Catholics and Jews are more likely to listen more often (at least once a week) than are the Protestant listeners. It should be noted, however, that the contingency coefficient is only .1530, indicating that though a relationship does exist it is not a very strong one. It is also recognized, however, that listening to a local radio station does not indicate that one is necessarily using the radio as a means to gain information on local affairs. It is possible that one who indicates that he listens is actually listening to music, weather, or traffic reports and is in fact paying little attention to actual local news reports. Respondents were, therefore, asked to indicate the approximate amount of their listening time devoted to local news. The following table indicates this data.

Relationship between religion and the amount of listening time devoted to local news by local radio listeners.

Religion	At Least Half	One-fourth	Less
Prot. (n = 57)	45.6%	42.1%	12.3%
Cath. (n = 118)	45.8	42.4	11.1
Jew. (n = 133)	51.1	42.1	6.8

$x^2 = 2.47$ NS 4df

Clearly, although religious group membership does play a significant role in determining the composition of the audience of the local radio station, it plays no significant role in the extent to which these listeners say they pay attention to local news broadcasts. Apparently, listeners of different religions devote about the same time to local news broadcasts.

The same test of exposure to the local media through the local radio can be run in relation to the various nationality groups within the Catholic community in Ramapo to ascertain the difference, if any, among Catholics in this area. It may be recalled that the nationality of the Catholic respondent made little difference in the vote analysis attempted in an earlier chapter. The table below presents the data.

Relationship between nationality and the frequency of local radio listening (among Catholics).

Nationality	At Least Once/Week	Less	Never
Irish (n = 34)	58.8%	17.6%	23.5%
Italian (n = 73)	58.9	1.4	39.7
German (n = 26)	61.5	19.2	19.2

$x^2 = 14.05$ P = .01 4df   C = .3091

It is interesting to note that nationality apparently plays a definite and significant role in determining the listening habits of Catholic respondents. While each of the three groups has approximately the same percentage of frequent listeners, a greater percentage of Italians never listen at all, while considerably more Germans listen to the local radio than any other Catholic group. In addition, the value of C (C = .3091) indicates a comparatively strong relationship. Once again it may be argued, however, that the data only indicate the frequency with which respondents set their dial to a local radio station, and not how often they listen to the local news reports. It is therefore necessary to test the extent to which Catholic radio listeners listen to local news reports on the radio with their nationality. The data are presented below.

The relationship between nationality and listening time devoted to local radio news (among Catholics).

Nationality	At Least Half	Less
Irish (n = 26)	46.1%	53.9%
Italian (n = 44)	52.2	47.8
German (n = 20)	55.0	45.0

$x^2 = .39$ NS 4df

Evidently, the Catholic community does not differ significantly, by nationality group, as to the amount of time devoted to local news reports. As was the case in regard to religion, while there are significant differences in the extent of who does or does not listen to the radio, once a respondent has made the decision to listen, his interest in local news operates independently from his ethnic identification.

One side comment is in order. The meaningful differences in relation to radio listening found among religious groups generally as well as within the Catholic community have a further implication: no significant differences exist in terms of the extent to which radio listeners listen to the local radio than do Protestants, and listeners of all groups listen to the local news to a similar degree, it follows that more Catholics and Jews listen to news on the local radio than do Protestants. This is also the case within the Catholic community. Italian Catholics are significantly less likely to listen to local radio than are Irish or German Catholics. Since it has been found that listeners of all three groups listen to the local news to a similar degree, it appears that fewer Italians listen to local news on the radio than Irish or Germans.

In addition to the local radio stations, respondents may be exposed to local affairs through the local press. Rockland County has three local newspapers: The Journal-News, The Independent, and The Record, each of which carries considerable news of local social, economic, and political affairs. In order to test the respondent's attention to local news it is therefore necessary to account for the frequency and intensity with which he reads the press. The following table presents this data related to religion.

Relationship between religion and the frequency of local newspaper reading.

Religion	At Least Once/Week	Less Often	Never
Prot. (n = 91)	79.1%	15.4%	5.5%
Cath. (n = 165)	73.9	18.2	7.9
Jew. (n = 208)	71.2	19.2	9.6

x^2 = 2.41 NS 4df

Clearly, no relationship exists between religion and the frequency of local newspaper reading. The overwhelming majority of each group claims to read the local newspaper often, only a negligible percentage (less than one-tenth) never read it at all. It has been found, however, that a significant relationship between religion and radio listening does exist. However, this relationship does not extend to the area of newspaper reading.

It may be that though religion does not relate to the frequency with which respondents read the local paper, it will relate to their reading habits in another sense. Perhaps significant differences exist in the extent to which newspaper readers of all groups read the local section of their paper. Indeed, such a test would more clearly ascertain the readers' interest in local affairs. The following table presents this data.

Relationship between religion and the tendency to read the local section of the local newspaper among local newspaper readers.

Religion	Read Local Section	Do Not Read Local Section
Prot. (n = 84)	78.6%	21.4%
Cath. (n = 152)	90.1	9.9
Jew. (n = 187)	88.2	11.8

$x^2 = 6.85$ P = .05 2df   C = .1261

As indicated above, there are significant differences in the reading habits of the various religious groups. Apparently, Catholics and Jews are more likely to read the local section of the local paper than are Protestants. It should be noted, however, that the value of C (.1261) for this relationship is not high, which implies a relatively low degree of association between religion and reading habits.

Two interesting comments may be derived from this data. The first relates to the nature of the ethnic groups being studied. It will be recalled that the present data regarding newspaper reading is not unlike that relating to radio listening. As indicated previously (see table on page 81); Catholic respondents claimed to be the most avid radio listeners, with Jews slightly less so and Protestants far less so. This finding is duplicated in the present data (see table on this page). Here, too, Catholics are slightly more likely to read the local section of the local newspaper than are Jews, while Protestants are considerably less so. By and large, it seems that Protestants are least likely to be exposed to the local media while Catholics claim to be most well informed.

The second comment relates more to the nature of religion as a variable. It was earlier found that religion significantly relates to the frequency with which respondents listen to the local radio. However, it was not found to relate to the listener's tendency to hear local news. In relation to the respondent's reading habits, just the opposite was found to be the case. There was no relationship between religion and the respondent's tendency to read the local paper. Nevertheless, among newspaper readers religion did relate significantly to the tendency to read the local section of the local paper.

It is suspected that this apparent discrepancy is not attributable to the nature of religion as a variable. It may be that while religion relates significantly to the frequency with which one listens to the local radio, it cannot relate to listening habits. Once a respondent has tuned to the local station, it is an unnecessary effort to change the channel to avoid the local news, especially if he intends to tune in again after the news. In most cases, it is simpler to leave the local station tuned and hear the news. Therefore, while religion may relate with the frequency of listening to the local station, local-news-listening may be more a matter of convenience and operate independently.

This is not the case with the newspaper. Here the contrary is true. Opening the local paper, glancing at it, or even having it in the house may have constituted "reading" it to respondents. This is especially true because many local residents have the local paper delivered. However, it requires a special effort to not only "read" the local paper but to read the local section. It is therefore quite consistent to find that religion as a variable related both to the frequency with which respondents listened to the local radio station and read the local section of the newspaper--both being the activities which require the greatest effort. It is therefore also quite consistent to find that in both these two areas not only did religion relate significantly but the results were quite similar; that is, Catholics were slightly more likely to read the local section of the local paper and to listen to the local radio than were Jews, while Protestants were considerably less so.

Given these findings, it would be interesting to test nationality for Catholics as a variable in this area. For instance, what is the relationship between nationality and the local reading habits of Catholic respondents? The table below presents this data.

Relationship between frequency of local newspaper reading and nationality among Catholic readers.

Nationality	At Least Once/Week	Less Often	Never
Irish (n = 35)	71.4%	14.2%	14.2%
Italian (n = 71)	76.1	15.5	8.5
German (n = 26)	65.4	26.9	7.7

x^2 = 2.97 NS 4df

Evidently, nationality plays no significant role in the tendency to read the local newspaper. This finding is not unlike that defined for religion; that is, the overwhelming majority of respondents read the local newspaper and this result is true across religious lines. Here, too, all Catholics tend to read the local newspaper in large numbers, and no significant difference is to be found along national lines.

It is still possible, however, that nationality will play a significant role in the tendency to read the local section of the local newspaper among Catholic readers. The material follows.

Relationship between nationality and the tendency to read the local section of the local newspaper among Catholics.

Nationality	Read Local Section	Do Not Read Local Section
Irish (n = 32)	93.8%	6.2%
Italian (n = 65)	86.2	13.8
German (n = 26)	80.8	19.2

x^2 = 2.23 NS 2df

As the data indicate, there is no significant relationship between nationality and the tendency to read the local section of the local newspaper. Clearly, nationality plays no significant role at all in the newspaper reading habits of the Catholic community of Ramapo.

To recapitulate, thus far it has been found that ethnicity does not play a major role in relation to the respondent's exposure to local affairs through the local media. The overwhelming majority of respondents from all groups claim to listen to local radio and read the local paper.

Certain minor differences between ethnic groups were noted, however. Nationality, for example, related significantly among Catholic respondents to the tendency to listen to local radio. German Catholic respondents were found to listen to the radio most often, while Italian Catholics were least likely to listen regularly.

Similarly, religion related significantly to the respondents' tendency to listen to local radio, as well as to their tendency to read the local newspaper. Jewish voters were most likely to listen to the local radio with regularity, while Catholic voters were most likely to indicate that they got their local news from the local newspaper.

The results generally indicate that the respondents' exposure to local media operates largely independently from ethnicity, defined either as religion or as nationality for Catholics. This may mean that ethnicity as such is unimportant in this area or it may imply that media exposure is a highly independent variable which relates to virtually no others. It remains, therefore, to test the relationship between exposure to the local media and other selected variables.

THE LOCAL MEDIA AND OTHER VARIABLES

Now that the role of ethnicity in the exposure of respondents to the local media has been ascertained, it is necessary to determine the importance of other variables in this area and to compare them to the findings relevant to ethnicity. It is first necessary to take note of a finding not anticipated. Either because exposure to the local media is not a vital element in the local political arena, or because of the great percentage of respondents who claim to read or listen to local news, or because subjects were less than candid in their responses few variables proved significant. These few will be presented and the strength of their relationship with the respondents' attention to the local media will be compared to those of ethnicity.

In terms of listening to the local radio, no variable other than religion proved significant. Thus, superficially, it might seem that one small part of the hypothesis has been confirmed: ethnicity is the most (indeed, the only) important variable in the determination of the respondents' exposure to local radio. The relationship however is suspect because it is the only significant relationship found and because the relationship with religion was not a strong one (alpha significant only at .05 and $C = .1530$). The suspicion is confirmed when control variables are applied to the relationship between religion and frequency of radio listening. Table 5.1 presents this data.

87

TABLE 5.1

Relationship Between Religion and Frequency of Radio
Listening When Occupation Is Held Constant

	Professional At Least		
Religion	Once/Week	Less Often	Never
Prot. (n = 15)	26.7%	40.0%	33.3%
Cath. (n = 28)	28.6	32.1	39.3
Jew. (n = 64)	45.3	14.1	40.6
$x^2 = 7.45$ NS 4df			

	White Collar At Least		
Religion	Once/Week	Less Often	Never
Prot. (n = 30)	26.7%	26.7%	46.7%
Cath. (n = 56)	46.4	28.6	25.0
Jew. (n = 71)	50.7	26.8	22.5
$x^2 = 7.51$ NS 4df			

	Skilled Labor At Least		
Religion	Once/Week	Less Often	Never
Prot. (n = 19)	36.8%	31.6%	31.6%
Cath. (n = 43)	32.6	30.2	37.2
Jew. (n = 40)	45.0	37.5	17.5
$x^2 = 4.11$ NS 4df			

	Unskilled Labor At Least		
Religion	Once/Week	Less Often	Never
Prot. (n = 21)	28.6%	47.6%	23.8%
Cath. (n = 31)	41.9	38.6	19.4
Jew. (n = 17)	23.5	47.1	29.4
$x^2 = 1.95$ NS 4df			

As the data indicate, the relationship between religion and the frequency with which respondents listen to
local radio disappears when occupation level is held in
control. At each level, the previously significant findings become insignificant. This may well indicate that
the relationship is spurious--the result of variables
other than religion and the local media. However, since
it is not likely that religion is "caused" by occupation,
it may also be that occupation acts as an intervening

variable in the relationship between religion and the
listening habits of respondents.

A similar effect may be noted when party affiliation
is held in control. Here again the previously significant
relationship between religion and frequency of radio listening disappears when party affiliation is held in control. Table 5.2 presents this.

TABLE 5.2

Relationship Between Religion and Frequency
of Radio Listening When Party
Affiliation Is Held Constant

| Religion | Republicans | | |
	At Least Once/Week	Less Often	Never
Prot. (n = 39)	35.9%	41.0%	23.1%
Cath. (n = 68)	36.8	33.8	29.4
Jew. (n = 39)	46.2	25.6	28.2
x^2 = 2.46 NS 4df			

| Religion | Democrats | | |
	At Least Once/Week	Less Often	Never
Prot. (n = 36)	27.8%	30.6%	41.7%
Cath. (n = 78)	42.3	28.2	29.5
Jew. (n = 133)	42.9	25.6	31.6
x^2 = 3.18 NS 4df			

Once again, it is evident that the relationship between religion and the listening habits of respondents
may well be spurious. Among both Republicans and Democrats, the previously significant relationship disappears.
It is again worthwhile to note, however, that since party
affiliation probably cannot "cause" religious identification, it is equally likely that party affiliation acts as
an intervening variable in the relationship between religion and the frequency with which respondents claim to
listen to local radio.

It will be recalled that, among Catholics, nationality was found to be significantly related to the listening
habits of respondents as well. Unfortunately, the distributions of the data do not permit an analysis of

nationality similar to that done above for religion. As
a result, it is not possible to determine the possible
spurious nature of the relationship. Therefore, it can
only be surmised that generally the frequency of radio
listening is a variable which operates more or less independently of any of the variables tested herein, as well
as ethnicity.

In terms of the extent to which local radio listeners
actually spent time listening to local news broadcasts,
it will be recalled that neither religion nor nationality
(for Catholics) proved significant in relation. In fact,
only one variable was found to be related: the respondent's attitude toward drug abuse. This data follows.

Relationship between listening time devoted to local
news and response to the statement: "Drug abuse is the
major issue facing our town."

Response	At Least One-half	One-fourth	Less
Agree (n = 183)	52.5%	38.3%	9.3%
No Opinion (n = 47)	38.3	40.4	21.3
Disagree (n = 99)	41.4	51.5	7.1

$$x^2 = 11.94 \quad P = .025 \ 4df \quad C = .1871$$

As the table indicates, those who have no opinion
are also those who spend time listening to local news.
Those most concerned about drug abuse are also those who
spend most time listening to local news. It is difficult
to determine the meaning and direction of this data, however. It must be recalled that at most these results
indicate association rather than causation. It is therefore difficult to decide whether these data indicate that
radio news has an effect upon the listeners' opinions, or
whether those with similar opinions tend to have similar
listening habits. In addition, the fact that this is the
only variable with a significant relationship in this
area leads one to believe that radio listening in general
is not a vital area of concern, is not a good index of
political interest, and acts independently from most of
the variables being herein tested.

The second local media in which exposure might indicate interest in local affairs are the local newspapers.
It was earlier shown that no significant relationship
existed between the frequency of local newspaper reading
and the religion of the respondent. The variable with
the strongest relationship to the reading habits of the
respondents was educational level. This data follows.

Relationship between education and frequency of local newspaper reading.

Education Level	At Least Once/Week	Less Often	Never
Non-H.S. Grad. (n = 27)	63.0%	18.5%	18.5%
H.S. Grad. (n = 141)	80.9	9.2	9.9
Some Col. (n = 124)	83.1	4.0	12.9
Col. Grad. (n = 127)	83.5	13.2	6.8

x^2 = 13.60   P = .05   C = .1772   6DF

As might be expected, a positive relationship exists between education and frequency of local newspaper reading; that is, the more education, the more likely is the respondent to read the local newspaper more frequently. (It must be noted references to "positive" or "negative" relationships here and elsewhere in this study are tentative at best. The author is well aware of the fact that with any other than 2 x 2 matrixes, it is quite possible for third variables to be so intertwined within the relationship as to create the illusion of positive-negative relationships when none really exists. The reader is therefore advised to understand such references in this study within the context of these remarks.) Nevertheless, it should be noted that at all levels, the large majority of respondents read the local newspaper often. The fact that the strongest relationship yielded so low a C value (C = .1772) also indicates that newspaper reading, like radio listening, acts more or less independently of most all other variables and is not a good index of local political interest or participation.

Finally, the exposure to local news through the newspaper is dependent upon the tendency of the respondent to read the local section of the paper. It was earlier indicated that religion did prove to be significant in relation to this variable. However, religion was not the most important variable. In this instance, occupation proved most significant. The following table presents this data.

Relationship between occupation and tendency to read the local section of the local paper.

Occupation	Read Local Section	Do Not Read Local Section
Professional (n = 105)	89.5%	10.5%
Wh. Collar (n = 140)	78.6	21.4
B. Collar (n = 87)	81.6	18.4
Unskilled (n = 73)	78.1	21.9

x^2 = 13.34   P = .05 6df   C = .1786

TABLE 5.3

Relationship Between Religion and the Tendency
to Read Local Section of Local Paper,
When Occupation Is Held Constant

	Professionals	
Religion	Read the Local Section	Do Not Read Local Section
Prot. (n = 14)	78.6%	21.4%
Cath. (n = 27)	88.9	11.1
Jew. (n = 61)	91.8	8.2

x^2 = 2.08 NS 2df

	White Collar	
Religion	Read the Local Section	Do Not Read Local Section
Prot. (n = 29)	75.9%	24.1%
Cath. (n = 53)	86.8	13.2
Jew. (n = 68)	83.8	16.2

x^2 = 1.65 NS 2df

	Skilled Labor	
Religion	Read the Local Section	Do Not Read Local Section
Prot. (n = 19)	84.2%	15.8%
Cath. (n = 40)	62.5	31.5
Jew. (n = 38)	92.1	7.9

x^2 = .88 NS 2df

	Unskilled Labor	
Religion	Read the Local Section	Do Not Read Local Section
Prot. (n = 20)	75.0%	25.0%
Cath. (n = 31)	96.8	3.2
Jew. (n = 18)	72.2	27.8

x^2 = 6.86   P = .05 2df   C = .3007

It is difficult to ascertain the meaning of this data, because it offers no clear direction. It was expected that a positive relationship would surface between occupation and reading habits, as was the previous case with education. This relationship did not surface, however, but rather an indeterminate one did. Professionals were most likely to read the local section, as expected, but blue-collar workers were next most likely, and all levels are quite likely to read the local section in any case. Here, too, it seems apparent exposure to the media is almost universal and few, if any, inferences can be made about it as an index of political interest.

Before leaving this area of the local media, however, one final point is in order. It was earlier noted that there is a significant relationship between religion and the tendency to read the local section of the local newspaper. The relationship, however, is not a strong one (alpha equals .05, C = .1261) and may well be spurious. Indeed, when occupation (the variable most important in this area) is held in control, the relationship between religion and reading habits disappears in all but one case.

It is evident that the earlier mentioned relationship between religion and the tendency to read the local section of the local paper is probably spurious. It is also notable that at the lowest occupation level Catholics are more likely to read the local section, while at all levels a large majority of each group is exposed to local news through the local paper. In sum, it may be reiterated that in Ramapo a very high number of residents are exposed to local news. Further, this operates more or less independently of socioeconomic, ethnoreligious, and political variables.

This leads the writer to one more conclusion. The very high number of respondents who are exposed to local news may indicate simply a high level of local political interest. Alternatively, it may be that exposure to local media is not a good index of local interest. The very sparsity of relationships found may support this conjecture. It remains yet to be seen whether relationships develop between these same variables and actual participation.

ACTUAL INTEREST-PARTICIPATION

Until now interest has been dealt with peripherally in terms of the exposure of the respondents to the local

media. In fact, Berelson has pointed out that the best
measure of political interest is the respondent's own estimation.[9] This question, together with the frequency of
the respondent's political discussions and whether or not
he voted in 1972, was asked.
    Relationship between religion and self-appraised po-
litical interest.

	Very		Not Very	Hardly
Religion	Interested	Interested	Interested	At All
Prot. (n = 86)	10.5%	41.9%	40.0%	8.1%
Cath. (n = 154)	11.7	43.5	38.3	6.5
Jew. (n = 192)	6.8	42.7	44.8	5.7

x^2 = 3.93 NS 6df

    As can can be plainly seen, there is virtually no
difference between various religious groups along the lines
of political interest, although Catholics claim to be very
slightly more interested and Jews slightly less interested.
Whatever differences surfaced, however, may well be attributed to randomness or differing standards of interest.
Much the same is the case among Catholic respondents as
regards national identity. This is shown below (it should
be noted that categories were collapsed to facilitate use
of the chi-square).
    Relationship between nationality and self-appraised
political interest, for Catholic respondents.

Nationality	Interested	Hardly At All
Irish (n = 34)	61.8%	38.2%
Italian (n = 67)	44.8	55.2
German (n = 22)	63.6	36.4

x^2 = 3.86 NS 2df

    As the figures indicate, although Italians are some-
what less interested in local politics, there is no significant difference between the nationality groups in this
area. Thus it appears that ethnicity is not a significant
variable in terms of self-estimated, local political interest.
    Lacking this relationship, the following question
must be: What, then, is significant in relation to self-
estimated political interest? Previous studies indicate
the great importance of party affiliations, and the
strength of party affiliation in determining the extent
of a citizen's interest.[10] These hypotheses have been
forwarded in the general political arena, however, and

have largely not been tested in the suburban political environment. As indicated below, party affiliation is significant in determining the extent of a respondent's interest, by his own estimation.

Relationship between party affiliation and self-avowed interest.

Party	Very Interested	Interested	Not Very Interested	Hardly At All
Rep. (n = 148)	13.5%	43.9%	33.1%	9.5%
Dem. (n = 268)	6.7	42.5	44.4	6.3

$$x^2 = 9.18 \quad P = .05 \text{ 3df} \quad C = .1469$$

Clearly, party affiliation is significant in determining political interest. In addition, the findings confirm most other findings in this regard--that Republicans are generally more interested in politics, albeit by their own estimation, than are Democrats. It should be noted, however, that the C value (C = .1469) is not a strong one. The most significant factor in determining interest, however, is intensity of party identification. The following table gives this story.

Relationship between the intensity of party affiliation and political interest.

Intensity	Very Interested	Interested	Not Very Interested	Hardly At All
Strong (n = 111)	25.2%	37.8%	34.2%	2.7%
Moderate (n = 253)	4.0	47.4	43.4	5.1
Weak (n = 91)	5.5	35.2	42.9	16.5

$$x^2 = 59.95 \quad P = .005 \text{ 6df} \quad C = .3406$$

As the data indicate, there is a positive relationship between intensity of party affiliation and political interest: those who identify most strongly with their party are more interested in politics than those whose identification is weakest.

It is also notable that those other variables which are usually defined as significant in terms of political interest are conspicuously nonsignificant in the present study. For example, it has been pointed out that a citizen's sense of efficacy--his feeling that he can effect change in the political system through some action--will be an important factor.[11] Thus, if a person feels that whatever he does changes will not result, he is not likely to pay much attention to what goes on. To test this sense

of efficacy, subjects were asked to respond to the following statement: "Generally speaking, it makes no difference whether the Republicans or Democrats are in control
in this town." They were also asked to respond to: "In
general, there is not much difference between the candidates for public office in this town." It is interesting
to note that both variables proved insignificant in correlation with self-estimated political interest ($x^2 = 11.27$
6df and $x^2 = 7.22$ 6df respectively).

In addition, it has been pointed out that the degree
of a citizen's trust for his government will also affect
his level of political interest significantly.[12] This
theory reasons that the citizen with little trust will pay
more attention to events and happenings, while the citizen
with a high degree of trust is more likely to leave governance to those in office, simply because he is satisfied
that they are doing a good job. To test this variable,
subjects were asked to respond to the following statement:
"In general, we can usually trust local officials to do
what is right." Once again, no significant relationship
was found in correlation with political interest ($x^2 = 9.44$
6df). It should be noted that these findings may not deny
the aforementioned hypotheses. Those with high levels of
efficacy may be paying attention to other than local affairs, in the belief that the real power to bring change
lies at a different governmental level. Equally, there is
no reason to argue that only those who mistrust government
will be interested in local affairs. Those who are satisfied with the status quo may be also interested in maintaining it and are therefore just as watchful. Indeed,
support and expectation are no less inputs than are demands.

It is recognized, however, that more objective measures of political interest and participation can be applied to study further the relationship between this di-
mension of political activity and ethnicity. Respondents
were also asked if they voted in 1972 and how often they
had local political discussions. Since the proportion of
those voting in Ramapo in 1972 was 84.5 percent (according
to the Rockland County Board of Elections), it was reasoned
that a respondent who claimed that he did not vote in 1972
probably did not vote regularly. Further, the frequency
of political discussions also indicates the degree to
which a respondent is interested in that which takes place
in his town. In addition, this latter element may also be
viewed as a means of exposure to local affairs, in the
"two-stepped" level of communications (from the media to

discussants and opinion leaders, and thence to the general electorate).[13] As the table below indicates, no significant relationship was discerned between religion and voting in 1972.

Religion	Voted	Did Not Vote
Prot. (n = 91)	78.0%	22.0%
Cath. (n = 167)	79.0	21.0
Jew. (n = 205)	85.9	14.1

$x^2 = 3.99$ NS 2df

Quite clearly, the overwhelming majority of each group voted in 1972, and this tendency to vote cuts across religious lines. This same effect is in evidence when religion is correlated to the frequency of local political discussions--that is, no significant correlation surfaces. The following table presents this data.

Religion	At Least Once/Week	Less Often	Never
Prot. (n = 90)	36.7%	32.2%	31.1%
Cath. (n = 162)	47.5	30.9	21.6
Jew. (n = 205)	48.8	31.7	19.5

$x^2 = 5.99$ NS 4df

As indicated, there is no significant relationship between religion and frequency of political discussions. It is interesting to note, nevertheless, that the direction of the findings is at odds with those indicated earlier. It was previously pointed out (see first table on page 94) that Jews claim to be the least interested in local affairs. The major differentiation lay at the "Very Interested" level in which were found 10.5 percent of the Protestant respondents, 11.7 percent of the Catholic respondents, but only 6.8 percent of the Jewish respondents. The last two tables, however, indicate that despite this claim, Jews voted in larger numbers and had somewhat more frequent political discussions than any other group, though it must be remembered that each or all of these distributions might well be random.

Several possible explanations exist for this apparent discrepancy. Perhaps some respondents were less than truthful--this possibility places the onus either upon the Christian respondents in terms of political interest or upon the Jewish respondents in terms of voting or frequency of local political discussions. Equally, it may be that

respondents did not differentiate in their minds between
local affairs and politics generally--this might mean
that subjects did not distinguish between general political interest and interest in local affairs, or between
political discussions and those regarding local affairs,
although in both cases they were requested to do so. Finally, there may exist different standards of interest
between Jews and non-Jews. Within the present context
this implies that Jews may be better informed or objec-
tively more interested in local affairs, yet consider their
interest to be inadequate in relation to some subjective
standard of political interest which is considerably higher
than that of non-Jews.

In fact, some evidence may be inferred (from the
first table on page 94) to support, tentatively, the third
proposition (though again it must be cautioned that none
of these tables reached the .05 level of significance).
The major difference between the groups there lay at the
"Very Interested" and "Not Interested" levels, which indicates that while about the same proportion of Jews and
non-Jews had some interest in politics, the distinction
lay in the highly subjective area of intensity, precisely
the one in which different standards would play the greatest role. In any event, such speculation must remain extremely tentative due to the nonsignificant nature of the
data.

Interestingly, the same was not true of the role of
nationality in relation to turnout. For example, significant differences were found within the Catholic community
as to the tendency to vote in 1972. This data follows.

Nationality	Voted	Did Not Vote
Irish (n = 35)	62.9%	37.1%
Italian (n = 73)	82.2	17.8
German (n = 26)	88.5	11.5

$$x^2 = 7.15 \quad P = .05 \ 2df \quad C = .2250$$

As is evident, Irish voters were far less likely to
vote in 1972 than were other Catholics, and Germans were
most likely. At first glance, it must be frankly admitted that no meaningful explanation for this phenonemon
could be proffered. Further testing, in fact, led to the
indication that the relationship might well be spurious.
Table 5.4 indicates the same relationship when party is
held constant.

TABLE 5.4

Relationship Between Nationality and Voter Turnout,
for Catholics, When Party Affiliation
Is Held in Control

Nationality	Republicans Voted	Did Not Vote
Irish (n = 13)	61.5%	38.5%
Italian (n = 34)	70.6	29.4
German (n = 10)	80.0	20.0

x^2 = .92 NS 2df

Nationality	Democrats Voted	Did Not Vote
Irish (n = 18)	66.7%	33.3%
Italian (n = 33)	84.9	15.1
German (n = 11)	90.9	9.1

x^2 = 3.46 NS 2df

Thus, while the direction of the relationship remained the same in both instances, the significance level dropped below the .05 level. Since party affiliation cannot cause nationality, it seems unlikely that this is a spurious relationship. Rather, it must at least be said that party affiliation represents an intervening variable.

Finally, it has been found (see the following data) that no significant relationship exists between nationality and the frequency of political discussions, for Catholics, just as no relationship is found between religion and the frequency of local political discussions.

Nationality	At Least Once/Week	Less Often	Never
Irish (n = 33)	42.4%	39.4%	18.2%
Italian (n = 71)	47.9	28.2	23.4
German (n = 24)	62.5	16.7	20.8

x^2 = 4.07 NS 4df

Once again, it appears that though the relationship is not a significant one, German Catholics are most actively interested in local politics, while Irish Catholics are least interested. Most important at this point is the fact that the hypothesis--the expected strong relationship between ethnicity and interest-participation in local politics--has not surfaced. It was earlier shown that party affiliation and, especially, the intensity of party affiliation are most significantly related to self-appraised local political interest. It now remains to decide what relates most strongly to voter turnout and frequency of political discussions, in the absence of ethnicity.

The findings regarding voter turnout proved to be somewhat unexpected. Many of the variables usually associated with the tendency to vote (as well as political interest generally) did not relate significantly with turnout. Thus the two measures of efficacy, political trust and intensity of party identification, were found to be insignificant (5.41 4df, .79 4df, 3.43 4df, and 3.72 2df respectively). Party affiliation was found to be significant although the value of C was not a strong one (C = .1439). Similarly, a significant relationship surfaced with education, but not one which carried a strong C value (C = .1844). In fact, the only variable which proved more strongly related to turnout than nationality, for Catholics, was occupation. The following table presents this data.

Occupation	Voted	Did Not Vote
Professional (n = 117)	93.2%	6.8%
Wh. Collar (n = 181)	86.2	13.8
Skilled Labor (n = 116)	75.0	25.0
Unskilled (n = 78)	61.5	38.5

$$x^2 = 36.73 \quad P = .005 \quad C = .2636$$

As might be expected, and as has been pointed out in previous studies, there is a positive relationship between occupation and turnout; that is, the higher status the occupation, the more likely is the respondent to vote. This finding pertains to the entire sample as a whole, however, while the relationship between nationality and turnout has only been tested for Catholic respondents in this study. It may be that this same strong relationship between nationality and turnout would appear among other ethnic groups. This would imply that ethnicity defined as national background has a significant and consistent impact upon turnout among all groups. Alternatively, it is possible that testing the relationship between nationality and turnout among non-Catholic voters would indicate

that the relationship found above is peculiar to the Catholic voter: nationality is significantly related to turnout only among Catholics. This would imply that separate
models of turnout behavior would have to be constructed
for Catholic and non-Catholic voters. Unfortunately, the
present data do not permit further analysis along these
lines.

A related test of the viability of nationality as a
variable in relation to turnout within the Catholic community is possible, however. It will be recalled that the
only variable which proved to have a higher C value than
nationality for Catholics was occupation--a variable which
was not limited to the Catholic community but which included all of the present sample. It would be interesting
therefore to relate nationality, for Catholics, to turnout
(holding occupation constant). Table 5.5 presents this
data--although it was necessary to combine occupational
categories in order to facilitate use of the chi-square
statistic and to eliminate zeroes.

TABLE 5.5

Relationship Between Nationality and Voter Turnout,
for Catholics, When Occupation Is Held Constant

Professional and White Collar		
Nationality	Voted	Did Not Vote
Irish (n = 16)	68.8%	31.2%
Italian (n = 42)	85.7	14.3
German (n = 14)	92.9	7.1
x^2 = 3.53 NS 2df		

Skilled and Unskilled Labor		
Nationality	Voted	Did Not Vote
Irish (n = 18)	55.6%	44.4%
Italian (n = 31)	77.4	22.6
German (n = 11)	81.8	18.2
x^2 = 3.36 NS 2df		

As the data indicate, the significance of the relationship between nationality and turnout for Catholic
respondents disappears when occupation is held constant.
Several inferences may be made here. Although no data

exists at present to indicate the importance of nationality to non-Catholics in relation to turnout, it is evident
that occupation level--the variable of greatest general
importance in this area--is quite significant to Catholics.
However, since occupation cannot "cause" nationality, it
seems equally evident that the relationship between nationality and turnout for Catholics is not spurious.
Rather, occupation level may serve as an intervening variable. This may also be the case for the non-Catholic
voter. Since data regarding the national backgrounds of
non-Catholics in the sample does not exist, no further
inferences can be presently made.

The final measure of political interest, frequency
of political discussions, was found to correlate most
strongly with intensity of partisan identification and
occupation, not an unexpected finding considering earlier
mentioned results relevant to voter turnout and self-
appraised political interest (see page 94). The following
tables present these two relationships.

Relationship between the intensity of party identification and the frequency of local political discussions.

| | At Least | | |
Intensity	Once/Week	Less Often	Never
Strong (n = 115)	60.0%	22.6%	17.4%
Moderate (n = 262)	41.6	36.3	22.1
Weak (n = 94)	37.2	36.2	26.6

$$x^2 = 14.56 \quad P = .005 \text{ 4df} \quad C = .1732$$

Relationship between occupation and frequency of political discussions.

| | At Least | | |
Occupation	Once/Week	Less Often	Never
Prof. (n = 117)	56.4%	28.2%	15.4%
Wh. Col. (n = 179)	45.8	34.1	20.1
Sk. Labor (n = 115)	42.6	31.3	26.1
Unskld. (n = 75)	32.0	34.7	33.3

$$x^2 = 14.91 \quad P = .025 \text{ 6df} \quad C = .1726$$

The data indicate a clearly positive relationship
between both variables and the frequency of local political discussions: as the intensity of partisan identification increases, so does the frequency of discussions.
Similarly, as the level of the respondent's occupational
status increases so does the frequency of political discussions. It must be noted that these findings were by no

means unexpected, and they confirm the direction of previous findings--both here and elsewhere--regarding the
role of partisan identification and class in the area of
political interest and participation.

INTEREST-PARTICIPATION IN THE SUBURBS: A SUMMARY

Several interesting findings have emerged from the
data regarding interest and participation in local politics. It has first been indicated that respondents are,
by and large, quite exposed to local affairs through the
local media. Not only do subjects claim to listen to the
local radio or read the local newspaper, but they also
indicate that a large portion of this reading and listening is devoted to local news and affairs. In addition,
this exposure has been found to be more or less independent of other variables here being tested; that is, few
significant relationships between exposure to local affairs and socioeconomic, ethnoreligious, political, or
attitudinal variables have emerged. Rather, it appears
that this attention to local affairs crosses these lines
and extends to most all segments of the local electorate.

Significant relationships did, however, emerge when
more direct measures of political interest and participation were applied. Respondents were asked to assess their
own political interest as well as to estimate the frequency with which they held political discussions with
friends and relatives. In addition, they were asked
whether they voted in 1972. In relation to these measures,
the intensity of the respondent's partisan affiliation as
well as his occupation were found to be significant. Generally, there was a positive relationship between occupation and interest-participation, as well as between intensity of partisan affiliation and interest-participation.
This confirms prior studies of interest generally; it also
indicates that many of the same variables operative in the
area of political participation are also significant in
the more limited case of the suburbs (to the extent that
Ramapo may be used as an example of a suburb).

Interesting for their absence were such oft studied
variables as efficacy and trust. Although earlier studies
indicated that a citizen would be most likely to participate if he felt that his actions would have an effect or
if he did not trust the incumbent leadership, these variables did not relate significantly to measures of participation here. A number of possible explanations come to

mind. It is possible that the generally high rate of interest and participation found in Ramapo obscures or crosses the usual lines of efficacy and trust. To this extent, Ramapo has confirmed the "hyperinvolvement" thesis of suburban political participation, and this great involvement--which is claimed to be largely socioeconomic and ecological in origin--overpowers the more personal and psychological variables of efficacy and trust.

It is equally possible that the results were more methodological than substantive in origin. Since the present study was not intended to delineate the importance of efficacy and trust in political participation, it is not unlikely that the items used to test these variables or the manner in which they were evaluated did not permit the type of comprehensive analysis required to study so complex a political variable. Therefore, it may be that efficacy and trust were operative but have not been properly measured in the present study.

Finally, it was found that ethnicity played a generally negligible role in the area of political interest. In most tests of exposure to local affairs, neither religion nor nationality was found to be significant for Catholic respondents. Subjects were quite attentive to local affairs across ethnoreligious lines. This should not be unexpected, since this was the general trend for this measure of participation, as noted above.

In the more direct area of actual participation, it was also found that ethnoreligious factors play no significant role. Once again it was found that respondents, by and large, participate in local affairs, and this participation crosses ethnoreligious lines. In addition, in those few areas in which significant relationships between ethnicity and participation did emerge, the relationships disappeared when controls--notably partisanship and socioeconomic status--were applied. In light of these findings, the earlier hypothesis regarding the importance of ethnicity in relation to local political participation and interest must be abandoned.

NOTES

1. A. Campbell et al., <u>The American Voter</u> (New York: John Wiley, 1960), chap. 5; B. Berelson et al., <u>Voting</u> (Chicago: University of Chicago, 1954), p. 26; Wm. Gannon, <u>Power and Discontent</u> (Homewood, Ill.: Dorsey, 1968); H. Hamilton, "The Municipal Voter: Voting and Non-Voting in

City Elections," <u>American Political Science Review</u> (December 1971): 1135-41.

2. R. Wood, "The Impotent Suburban Vote," <u>Nation</u> (March 26, 1960): 273; W. Martin, "The Structure of Social Relationships Engendered by Suburban Residence," <u>American Sociological Review</u> (August 1956); Wm. Dobriner, <u>Class in Suburbia</u> (Englewood Cliffs: Prentice-Hall, 1963), chap. 1.

3. Wm. Whyte, <u>The Organization Man</u> (New York: Simon & Schuster, 1956); H. Wattel, "Levittown: A Suburban Community," in Wm. Dobriner, ed., <u>The Suburban Community</u> (New York: Putnam, 1958).

4. B. Berger, <u>Working-Class Suburb</u> (Berkeley: University of California, 1960), pp. 36ff.

5. H. Douglas, "The Suburban Trend," in Dobriner, <u>The Suburban Community</u>, op. cit., p. 308.

6. S. Donaldson, <u>The Suburban Myth</u> (New York: Columbia University, 1969), see especially p. 157.

7. Ibid., pp. 155-56; Wood, op. cit.; D. Reisman, "The Suburban Sadness," in Dobriner, <u>The Suburban Community</u>, op. cit., especially pp. 375-80.

8. Campbell, op. cit., chap. 5; Hamilton, op. cit., n. 1.

9. See, for example, B. Berelson et al., <u>The People's Choice</u> (New York: Columbia University, 1968), pp. 40-41.

10. See Campbell et al., op. cit., pp. 96-101; also Wm. Flanagan, <u>Political Behavior of the American Electorate</u> (Boston: Allyn and Bacon, 1967).

11. A. Campbell et al., <u>The Voter Decides</u> (Evanston, Ill.: Row, Peterson & Co., 1954); Hamilton, op. cit., p. 1136; A. Ranney and L. Epstein, "The Two Electorates," <u>Journal of Politics</u> (August 1966): 598-616.

12. Gannon, op. cit.; also, J. Fraser, "The Mistrustful-Efficacious Hypothesis and Political Participation," <u>Journal of Politics</u> (May 1970): 444-49; also B. Hawkins, U. Marando, and G. Taylor, "Efficacy, Mistrust and Political Participation," <u>Journal of Politics</u> (February 1969): 1130-36.

13. See Campbell, <u>The American Voter</u>, op. cit., chap. 5; also Flanagan, op. cit., p. 43.

CHAPTER

6

**TOWARD
A THEORY**

The previous three chapters have largely presented the data and analyzed those areas in which ethnicity did or did not relate significantly to a given area of suburban politics. The three subareas--voting, attitudes, and participation--were dealt with more or less independently, although a general context of ethnicity in the suburbs was maintained. In this chapter, a comprehensive causal theory will be attempted to explain and coordinate the findings of this study. Various models will be studied, and the best alternatives will be developed and expanded upon.

DISCERNING A CAUSAL PATTERN

It will be recalled that ethnicity was found to be a significant variable in voting only when defined as religion. This relationship between religion and voting was found to exist at all electoral levels. However, religion was found to be less important in relation to the vote than party affiliation and racial attitude. The respondent's party affiliation related most strongly to the vote at all electoral levels. The attitude toward residential segregation was second most important. These three variables, then, party affiliation, religion, and racial attitude will be utilized as the main determinants of the vote for Ramapo residents in 1972.

In order to present the possible causal progressions of the present data graphically, a model was constructed in the third chapter. In order to facilitate the present discussion, it would be well to re-create that figure here. This is done below.

106

FIGURE 6.1

The Ramapo Vote

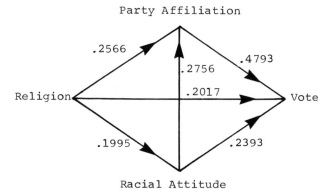

As Figure 6.1 indicates, religion has been chosen as
the first in the progression toward the vote based upon
the common-sense assumption that neither party affiliation
nor racial attitude cause the respondent to choose a particular religion. It is recognized that some movement may
take place within religious groups--as between denomina-
tions--based upon these two variables. However, this does
not affect the present case.

It will also be noted that Figure 6.1 includes a
series of C values which link the various elements. This
was not done in Chapter 3 because the relevant data had
not as yet been presented. It will be recalled that the
model was utilized in Chapter 3 only after certain qualifications were made explicit. Among these was the possibility that each or some of the variables operated independently from the others, and therefore no causal model
including all three could be devised. This qualification
may now be eliminated. It has been demonstrated that all
three variables not only relate significantly to the vote
but also relate significantly to each other. The several
values listed in the figure give a clue to the strength
of these relationships. An attempt will be made, by the
means of statistical control, to decide the succession of
variables to the vote. (It should be noted that the coefficients appearing in the diagram are means computed
from the five elections under discussion. For the actual
C values of each election for each relationship, please
see Chapter 3.)

A note here is in order regarding the attempt to derive causal explanations from statistical findings. In Chapter 3, it was stated that the coefficients herein utilized were measures of association rather than causality. This implied that though relationships might be found for two given variables, the direction of these relationships--that is, which preceded or caused the other--could not be inferred from the data. Such inference may be possible when statistical controls are applied; for instance, by holding a third variable constant.[1]

Although the method is useful and aids inference, it has severe limitations. When two variables which have been found to relate significantly with each other are tested again with some third variable held in control, two important results may occur. The new relationship (A x B controlling for C) may still yield a significant relationship. In this case it would not be unreasonable to assume that the relationship earlier found (A x B) is not significantly related to the third variable (C). However, if it should be found that the new relationship (A x B controlling for C) falls to an insignificant level, there is virtually no way of determining whether this is an indication of the spuriousness of the original relationship (A x B) or an indication of the intervening nature of the third variable (C). In effect, such a finding may imply that the earlier relationship (A x B) was a result of the joint causal impact of the third variable and hence spurious. It may also imply that the original relationship operates through the third variable (A is still related to B but through C).

The difficulty lies in the fact that the present method does not indicate which of the two possible inferences is the correct one. In some instances, inference may be made upon some common-sense assumptions not unlike the proposition that religion is caused by neither party affiliation nor by racial attitude. The data are often too complex for such facile assumptions, however, and it must be recalled that such assumptions are in no way statistically based. Nevertheless, they must be utilized in pursuing the present analysis. In the words of one authority: ". . . the decision that a partial correlation is or is not spurious (does or does not indicate a causal ordering) can in general only be reached if a priori assumptions are made that certain other causal relations do not hold. . . ."[2]

Another qualification to be made regarding the present method relates to its lack of exclusivity. No matter

which variables are assumed to precede others, no causal
path excludes the simultaneous operation of others.
Therefore, if it is found that the relationship between
party affiliation and the vote becomes insignificant when
religion is held in control, it will be assumed that religion intervenes in the relationship between party affiliation and the vote. This, of course, is an a priori assumption, for it could just as properly be assumed that
the results indicate that the relationship between party
affiliation was a spurious one. In any event, the proposition that party affiliation operates in an indirect
manner in its relationship with the vote via religion
does not exclude the possibility, however, that religion
also operates in relation to the vote independently from
party affiliation. Therefore, whatever possibilities are
presented to explain the present data, it must also be
considered that the possibilities are to be studied in
combination with--as well as exclusive to--each other.

Let us now present a possible model of the vote,
keeping these various qualifications in mind, and test it
by controlling for third variables. A quick glance at
Figure 6.1 will show the reader that according to the
values of C alone, it seems that party affiliation has
the strongest direct relationship with the vote, racial
attitude is the next strongest, and religion is last.
Again it is assumed that though there may be other variables which relate to the vote, their effect will be
largely random.[3] It is reasonable to start our analysis
with the possibility that the causal model follows the
magnitude of the contingency coefficients; that is, that
religion will be most remote from the vote, while racial
attitude will be one step closer, and party affiliation
the closest. This model is presented in Figure 6.2.

If this model is to be used to explain the sequen-
tial relationship between the three variables under discussion and the vote, the following should be expected:

1. The relationship between party affiliation and
the vote will remain significant when racial attitude is
held in control;

2. The relationship between party affiliation and
the vote will remain significant when religion is held in
control;

3. The relationship between racial attitude and the
vote will not be significant when party affiliation is
held in control;

4. The relationship between racial attitude and the
vote will remain significant when religion is held in
control;

5. The relationship between religion and the vote will not be significant when party affiliation is held in control;

6. The relationship between religion and the vote will not be significant when racial attitude is held in control.

FIGURE 6.2

The Ramapo Vote: A Tentative Model

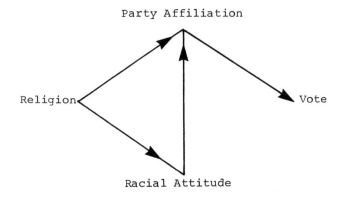

Each of these six relationships was tested to ascertain the viability of this first model. The following table presents the x^2 and C values for item 1.[4]

Results of tests distinguishing the relationship between party affiliation and the vote when racial attitude is held in control, 1df. Statement: "I see nothing wrong with Black people moving onto this block."

Election	Agree		No Opinion		Disagree	
	x^2	C	x^2	C	x^2	C
Pres.	42.40	.5108	37.09	.4722	10.23	.2881
Cong.	29.97	.4939	43.09	.4989	24.35	.4255
State Sen.	28.41	.4404	46.34	.5200	20.13	.4025
C'ty Sher.	19.67	.3755	48.54	.5273	10.99	.3147
T'n Just.	28.48	.4427	51.68	.5423	24.26	.4382

As the data clearly show, the relationship between party affiliation and the vote remains significant at all electoral levels, no matter what the subjects' response to the item on residential segregation. In addition,

in most cases the C value for each relationship remained
around or near the mean coefficient for the simple relationship between party affiliation and the vote (.4793).
It seems that item 1 has been confirmed; that is, party
affiliation is not significantly affected by racial attitude in the party's relationship with the vote.

Item 2 dealt with the relationship between party affiliation and the vote when religion was held in control.
It was postulated that if party affiliation has the most
direct relationship with the vote, then no significant
impact should be noticed when religion is held in control.
The following table indicates this to be the case.

Relationship between party affiliation and the vote
when religion is held constant, 1df.

Election	Protestant		Catholic		Jewish	
	x^2	C	x^2	C	x^2	C
Pres.	18.54	.4427	32.30	.4347	47.81	.4674
Cong.	30.27	.5339	32.21	.4347	33.71	.4049
State Sen.	30.30	.5413	25.91	.4062	35.40	.4183
C'ty Sher.	16.58	.4375	33.11	.4490	29.85	.3910
T'n Just.	9.32	.3492	52.33	.5311	44.47	.4645

Once again it seems that party affiliation is more
closely related to the vote than other variables.   In
each election, among each religious group, party affiliation remains a significant factor in relation to the vote.
Also, the C value remains close to the mean coefficient
found for the simple association of party affiliation to
the vote.   The first part of this first model has been
confirmed; that is, party affiliation has a direct relationship with the vote.   Neither religious identification
nor the respondent's attitude regarding residential segregation intervene in this relationship.

The fact that this has been found to be the case
does not, however, eliminate the possibility that either
religion or racial attitude also relate directly with
the vote.   The proposed model, however, implies that
party affiliation is the only variable with a direct relationship with the vote; that is, with which no other
variable intervenes.   Therefore, items 3 and 5 must be
tested: is there a significant relationship between
racial attitude or religion and the vote when party
affiliation is held in control?   The following table
shows the results.

Relationship between racial attitude and the vote
when party affiliation is held constant, 2 df.   Statement:

"I see nothing wrong with Black people moving onto this block."

Election	Republicans		Democrats	
	x^2	C	x^2	C
Pres.	1.74 - NS	-	31.02	.3275
Cong.	2.25 - NS	-	4.13 - NS	-
State Sen.	0.51 - NS	-	4.40 - NS	-
C'nty Sher.	4.44 - NS	-	13.30	.2231
T'n Just.	9.39	.2514	11.16	.2063

As the data indicate, the relationship between racial attitude and the vote becomes insignificant in a majority of cases when party affiliation is held constant. In addition, in each of those cases in which racial attitude remains significant, the value of C drops. For the simple relationship between racial attitude and the vote, the value of C was .3426 for the presidential election, .2677 for that of sheriff, and .2981 for that of town justice. A quick glance at the previous table shows the reader that the value has dropped in each case.

A point may also be in order in reference to the Democratic vote. Despite the fact that the C value has dropped in each case of significance, it is still interesting that racial attitude seems to have an unexpected tenacity in relation to the vote. This may have something to do with the temporal characteristics of the present data. Since the analysis is relating political attitudes to the 1972 election, the nature of this election must also be considered. The great Nixon landslide must have taken a toll on those who normally voted Democratic. It will be recalled that 38.7 percent of the respondents who claimed to be Democrats also reported that they had voted for Nixon (see Chapter 3). The present data may imply that the cutting edge for those who left the Democratic for the Republican slate was the race issue. Therefore, racial attitude has proved to have an electoral impact even when party affiliation is held in control, especially for Democrats. Nevertheless, even for Democrats, racial attitude loses some of its salience when party is held constant. It seems that party affiliation relates more directly with the vote than does racial attitude.

It is now necessary to test the relationship between religion and the vote when party affiliation is held in control. The following table shows the results of such a test.

Relationship between religion and the vote when party affiliation is held constant, 2df.

Election	Republicans		Democrats	
	x^2	C	x^2	C
Pres.	Unreliable	6	6.61	.1621
Cong.	2.15 – NS	–	3.24 – NS	–
State Sen.	0.51 – NS	–	6.99	.1679
C'nty Sher.	1.47 – NS	–	2.06 – NS	–
T'n Just.	6.61	.2224	3.71 – NS	–

Here, too, it seems evident that the relationship between party affiliation and the vote is stronger than that between religion and the vote. In the majority of cases, the relationship between religion and the vote becomes insignificant when party affiliation is held constant.

The fact that in some instances here, as well as in selected cases in the table for racial attitude related to the vote holding party affiliation in control (see p. 112) the relationships remain significant may be helpful in an earlier mentioned manner, however. It was noted that if a relationship is significant when two variables are studied (A x B) but becomes insignificant when a third is introduced (A x B controlling for C), this may indicate one of two things. It may indicate that the original relationship between (A) and (B) was solely a result of the effects of (C) on both and therefore spurious. It may equally indicate that the relationship between (A) and (B) is an indirect one which operates through (C). There is virtually no way to determine which of the possible explanations is the correct one without making certain a priori assumptions about the nature of the variables; assumptions--it may be added--that are not supportable by the data at hand.

The present case, however, may permit a determination that is at least suggested by the data. It has been found that religion and racial attitude each become insignificant variables in relation to the vote when party affiliation is held constant, in most cases. While, strictly speaking, this could mean that the original relationships were spurious and totally a function of the effects of party affiliation, the fact that the relationships remain significant in a minority of cases suggests otherwise. It does not seem unreasonable to assume that, since both religion and racial attitude remain significant in relation to the vote when party affiliation is held in control, the original relationships were not spurious. Rather, party affiliation intervenes in these relationships. It is recognized that though this inference must still be relegated to the world of assumptions, it is at least one that may be suggested by the data and is not purely a priori.

It has so far been indicated that party affiliation is the only one of the three variables being studied which has a direct relationship with the vote. The proposed model implied also that the relationship between religion and the vote was a less direct one than the relationship between racial attitude and the vote. Therefore, items 4 and 6 must be tested: does the relationship between religion and the vote become insignificant when racial attitude is held constant, and does the relationship between racial attitude and the vote remain significant when religion is held constant? The first of these relationships is tested below.

Relationship between religion and the vote when racial attitude is held constant, 2df. Statement: "I see nothing wrong with Black people moving onto this block."

Election	Agree		No Opinion		Disagree	
	x^2	C	x^2	C	x^2	C
Pres.	2.85–NS	–	6.26	.2135	4.77–NS	–
Cong.	1.01–NS	–	9.78	.2627	7.65	.2420
State Sen.	8.76	.2485	0.08–NS	–	2.20–NS	–
C'ty Sher.	1.96–NS	–	4.58–NS	–	2.05–NS	–
T'n Just.	7.14	.2307	5.72–NS	–	3.75–NS	–

The table seems to indicate that racial attitude intervenes in the relationship between religion and the vote. In 10 of 15 possible cases, religion does not relate significantly with the vote when racial attitude is held in control. The fact that it does remain significant in one-third of the cases again suggests that the original relationship (between religion and the vote) is not purely a function of racial attitude but is rather an indirect one in which racial attitude intervenes. It now seems that religion operates through both racial attitude and party affiliation and does not generally carry on a significant direct relationship with the vote.

The following table tests the final implication of the proposed model: that racial attitude will remain significant in relation to the vote when religion is held constant. This would mean that religion does not intervene in the relationship.

Relationship between racial attitude and the vote when religion is held constant, 2df. Statement: "I see nothing wrong with Black people moving onto this block."

Election	Protestants		Catholics		Jews	
	x^2	C	x^2	C	x^2	C
Pres.	4.68-NS	–	18.76	.3296	9.84	.2192
Cong.	6.25	.2602	12.35	.2741	1.55-NS	–
State Sen.	2.34-NS	–	7.27	.2184	5.01-NS	–
C'ty Sher.	4.70-NS	–	10.09	.2543	10.73	.2312
T'n Just.	10.56	.3515	12.57	.2807	10.73	.2336

The results presented above are ambiguous and difficult to interpret. On the one hand, it appears that the relationship between racial attitude and the vote remains significant in a majority of cases in which religion is held constant. The relationship remains significant in 10 of 15 possible instances. On the other hand, the relationship does become insignificant in five of the cases, and the value of C is decreased in three of the remaining cases. The original C values for the simple relationship between racial attitude and the vote were: presidential election: C = .2881; congressional election: C = .220; state senatorial election: C = .1646; sheriff election: C = .2402; and town justice election: C = .2835. A glance at the table above will show that C is decreased for Jews at the sheriff level and for Catholics and Jews at the town justice level.

Even more striking, however, is an apparent difference between the three religious groups. If Protestants and Jews are studied alone, it may be argued that religion serves as an intervening variable in the relationship between racial attitude and the vote. Of the ten possible cases, the relationship between racial attitude and the vote becomes insignificant in five, while the C value drops in two of the remaining five. Not so among Catholics. Racial attitude remains significant in each of the five elections for Catholics. In addition, in only one-- town justice--does the C value decrease. In fact, the value of C increases in each of the other four! It seems that racial attitude is a more salient electoral factor for Catholics than for Jews or Protestants.

That Catholics should be unique in measures of political attitudes, while Jews and Protestants are more similar to each other, is not a novel finding. In several studies of "public-regardedness," that is, the tendency to have political attitudes favoring public benefit

rather than parochial-sectarian benefit, Banfield and
Wilson found that Jews were closest to the "Yankee"
(Anglo-Saxon Protestant) ethos of "public-regardedness,"
while Catholic subjects were most likely to be "private-
regarding."[5]

It is interesting, however, that the present finding
somewhat contradicts other prior results. In Chapter 4
it was indicated that though there were significant differences between the religious groups in the area of residential segregation, the differences between Catholics
and Protestants were slight, while the attitudes of Jewish
respondents were quite distinct. These data are re-created
below to facilitate the discussion.

Relationship between religion and racial attitude.
Statement: "I see nothing wrong with Black people moving
onto this block."

Religion	Agree	No Opinion	Disagree
Prot. (n = 91)	30.8%	30.8%	38.5%
Cath. (n = 166)	31.9	30.7	37.3
Jew. (n = 205)	49.3	29.3	21.4

As the table indicates, Protestants and Catholics
differ by less than 2 percent in each category. Jews,
however, are considerably more favorable toward residential integration, they differ from Catholics and Protestants by over 15 percent. This is a virtual duplicate of
Campbell's findings regarding the attitudes of the various religious groups in the general area of race relations.[6] What is novel about the present findings relates
to the fact that though Catholics may be similar to Protestants in their racial attitudes, Catholics are considerably more likely to act upon these attitudes when they
go to the polls. In simple terms, no matter what orientation a group has, this remains academic unless it has an
effect on the vote. Apparently, race has a greater effect upon the Catholic vote than upon the vote of other
religious groups in the sample.

Based upon the tests executed to analyze the proposed
model of suburban voting and the impact of religion on the
vote, it now seems necessary to devise two distinct models.
One will accommodate the vote of Catholic respondents,
while the second will deal with the vote of the Protestant
and Jewish respondents. Before presenting these two models, it would be well to add one more caveat. It will be
recalled that in none of the instances in which it was expected that relationships which were previously significant

would become insignificant did this universally occur. For example, to test the viability of the proposed model it was expected that religion would not relate significantly with the vote if party affiliation were held constant. This was used to suggest that the original relationship was indirect rather than spurious.

This finding may be also used in another regard. The very fact that religion and/or racial attitude are significantly related in a minority of instances, despite the use of controls, indicates that though the relationship operates through an intervening variable, it also operates (albeit inconsistently and somewhat weakly) directly. This refers to a prior qualification regarding simultaneous causality. It was earlier mentioned that one causal inference is not exclusive of others. Therefore, the fact that party affiliation carries on a direct relationship with the vote does not negate the possibility that other variables do too. The fact that each variable maintains a significant relationship with the vote under controlled circumstances implies this.

The new models of voting behavior must account for this simultaneous causality while still indicating that certain relationships are more consistently direct than others. The models must also indicate that certain variables operate primarily in an indirect manner but in a (weakened) direct one as well. This can be done by the use of both an unbroken causal line--to indicate a consistent causal path--and a dotted line--to indicate a weakened and inconsistent causal path. Figure 6.3 presents a revised model for the activity of Protestant and Jewish voters in the sample.

As the figure indicates, both religion and racial attitude relate to the vote in an inconsistent fashion when controls are applied. The only consistently significant variable in relation to the vote is party affiliation. Both religion and racial attitude also relate to the vote indirectly through party affiliation. Finally, religion and racial attitude intervene with each other in relation to the vote.

It should be noted that all causal inference refers to the relationship with the vote. The fact that causal arrows have been drawn from religion to party affiliation, for example, is not meant to imply that religion causes party affiliation. It merely means that the path from religion to the vote goes through party affiliation, and it has been demonstrated that a relationship exists both between religion and the vote and between religion and party

117

affiliation. In order to study the causal effects of religion on party affiliation, control tests similar to
those employed in reference to the vote would be necessary. This is largely beyond the scope of the present
study, though some analysis of the implications of the
model in this regard will be made later. That only causality in reference to the vote is here implied, however,
should be borne in mind.

FIGURE 6.3

The Protestant and Jewish Vote

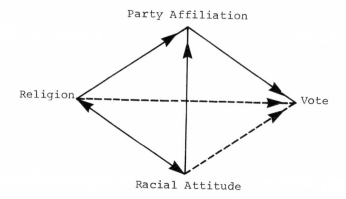

A second model is needed to accommodate the voting
habits of Catholic respondents. It will be recalled that
for Catholics, religion did not intervene in the relationship between racial attitude and the vote. This suggested
the greater importance of racial attitudes to the Catholic
voter. It should also be recalled, however, that this was
as the very original model implied (see above).
Therefore, the Catholic model will be essentially similar
to the original model except for the introduction of
dotted lines to indicate the inconsistent and weakened
nature of the relationships between religion and the vote,
as well as racial attitude and the vote under controlled
circumstances. Figure 6.4 presents this model.

As the figure indicates, both religion and racial attitude have a weakened and inconsistent relationship with
the vote. Only party affiliation carries on a consistently significant relationship with the vote. However,

whereas in the Protestant-Jewish model two-headed causal
arrows were drawn between religion and racial attitude to
indicate the mutually intervening nature of their relationship with the vote, here the causal path moves only
from religion to racial attitude, to indicate that for
the Catholic respondent religion did not intervene in the
relationship between racial attitude and the vote. Finally, both religion and racial attitude operate through
party affiliation in an indirect relationship with the
vote. This last causal path is the strongest and most
consistent one of all.

FIGURE 6.4

A Model for the Catholic Vote

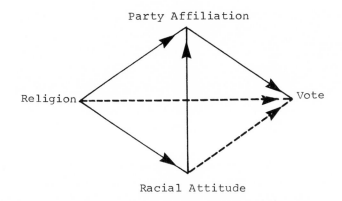

CAUSALITY: DISCUSSION AND INFERENCE

The two models of suburban ethnic voting behavior
represent an unexpected role for religion in differen-
tiating between the Catholic and Protestant-Jewish vote.
The fact that racial attitude has proven to be a more
salient political factor for Catholics than for others
is a novel finding which is fraught with implications and
open to varying interpretations. Some of these, and the
empirical evidence which they require, can be discussed
in this final section.

It should first be noted that though it has not
been generally theorized that racial attitude is more

politically significant for Catholics than for non-Catholics, it has been found that race is an important issue for the Catholic voter. Greeley, quoting a 1963 survey of Catholics, indicated that 51.3 percent of the respondents "scored high on racism." Among these, Polish Catholics scored highest and Italians second, with 61 percent and 54 percent respectively.[7] The internal convulsions over the race issue within the Catholic church, and the special difficulties of Black Catholics, have been graphically portrayed by Wakin and Scheuer.[8] Moynihan and Glazer, in analyzing the politics of race in New York City, conclude:

> The opponents of this coalition (white, liberal and pro-Black) can once again be described in ethnic and class terms. . . . Whether we say "blue-collar" or "lower-middle class" or "homeowner" in New York City, or whether we say "Italian" or "Irish" is not unimportant, and yet we know we are talking about the same people.[9]

The intent here, however, is not to determine the precise anchoring of Catholic racial attitudes, although that has been studied in Chapter 4. Rather, the author will attempt to explain and explore reasons for the pronounced importance of racial attitude to the Catholic voter.

One possible explanation may lie in an alternative interpretation of the data. The analysis thus far has proceeded under the assumption that because religion did not intervene in the relationship between racial attitude and the vote for Catholic respondents--whereas it often did for others--this implies that racial attitude is more salient to the Catholic. It may, alternatively, imply that religion is less important to the Catholic voter. This would explain the impotence of religion as an intervening variable for the Catholic voter. If this is the case, then, it would be edifying to see which voters indicated a stronger identification with their religious-ethnic communities. The hypothesis would suggest that Catholic voters are less strongly identified with their religious groups and therefore are not as affected as Protestants and Jews by this affiliation. These data follow.

Relationship between religion and intensity of religious identification.

Religion	Strong	Moderate	Weak
Catholic (n = 133)	24.1%	53.4%	22.6%
Prot. & Jew. (n = 209)	13.9	57.4	28.7

$$x^2 = 6.12 \qquad P = .05 \; 2df \qquad C = .1326$$

Catholics have been compared to Protestants and Jews as a group because this is what the proposed voting models imply. As the data indicate, there is a significant difference between Catholics and Jews and Protestants in terms of the intensity of religious identification. The results, however, are the contrary from what might be expected if religion were less important to the Catholic voter. Apparently, the Catholic voter is more strongly identified with his religion than are his Protestant and Jewish neighbors. It seems unlikely that the earlier findings relating to the weakness of religion as an intervening variable between racial attitude and the Catholic vote imply the lesser importance of religion to the Catholic.

Another inference from the data may relate to the intensity of party affiliation. It may be argued that the reason for the salience of racial attitude of the Catholic voter is somehow related to his degree of party affiliation. If it were found that the Catholic identifies with his party less intensely than do others, it may imply that there is a greater opportunity for particular issues to influence the Catholic voter--in this case the race issue. The possibility that party affiliation may account for the differences between Catholic and other voters is further suggested by the overwhelming importance of party affiliation--both in terms of magnitude of the C values and in terms of consistency--as compared to the other variables in relation to the vote. This hypothesis is tested below by comparing religion with intensity of party affiliation for Catholics and Protestants and Jews.

Relationship between religion and intensity of party affiliation.

Religion	Strong	Moderate	Weak
Catholics (n = 160)	24.4%	54.4%	21.3%
Prot. & Jew. (n = 281)	24.2	55.9	19.9

$$x^2 = .12 \; NS \; 2df$$

As the data indicate, there is virtually no difference between Catholics, Jews, and Protestants in terms of intensity of party identification. It seems that the greater importance of racial attitude for Catholics cannot be explained in terms of intensity of party affiliation.

Still another alternative may be related to socioeconomic status. It may be argued that the supposed importance of racial attitude for the Catholic voter is in fact not so much a function of Catholic identity as of socioeconomic factors which are related to the Catholic voter. Such a hypothesis would require that significant differences be found between the occupational and educational statuses of Catholics, Protestants, and Jews. The data, as related to education, follow.

Relationship between religion and education.

Religion	Col. Grad.	Some Col.	H.S. Grad.	Some H.S.
Cath. (n=164)	23.2%	32.3%	35.4%	09.1%
Prot. & Jew.				
(n=298)	32.6	29.5	30.9	07.0

$x^2 = 4.70$ NS 3df

As the table shows, some differences exist between Catholics and others in terms of education. In general, Catholic respondents are somewhat less likely to have received a higher education. However, these differences are not significant, and therefore they cannot be used to confirm the hypothesis that the importance of racial attitude to the Catholic voter is largely a function of education. A similar test regarding the occupational status of Catholics as compared to Jews and Protestants is somewhat more difficult to dismiss. The following table presents this.

Relationship between religion and occupational status.

Religion	Prof.	Wh. Col.	Skld Lab.	Unskld Lab.
Cath. (n = 164)	17.1%	36.0%	26.8%	20.1%
Prot. & Jew.				
(n = 289)	27.7	36.7	22.1	13.5

$x^2 = 8.81$ $P = .05$ 3df $C = .1382$

As the data indicate, there is significant difference between religion and occupational status when Catholics are compared to Protestants and Jews. Apparently, Catholic respondents were less likely to be in professional or white-collar occupations and more likely to be

skilled or unskilled laborers. Although the chi-square
value is significant at the .05 level, however, attention
is also called to the value of C (.1382). This is a
rather weak relationship and may well lend suspicion to
the entire finding.

If it is to be assumed that the Catholic tendency to
give greater political salience to racial attitude can be
explained in socioeconomic terms, as the occupational
data may suggest, further tests are required. It has already been shown that Catholics do not differ significantly from others in terms of education, and even the present
significant finding relating to occupation has yielded a
weak relationship. To confirm the socioeconomic hypothesis further, it might also be expected that Catholics
differ from both Jews and Protestants individually to a
significant degree. If it would be found, for example,
that when Jewish respondents are removed from the data
and Catholics are compared directly to Protestants no
significant occupational differences emerge, this would
further weaken the data. Such a finding would suggest
that the unique group, the group from whom we would expect unique voting data, was the Jewish rather than the
Catholic group. Conversely, if significant differences
emerge when Catholics are compared to Jews and to Protestants individually, this would strengthen the hypothesis
that the salience of racial attitude in the Catholic vote
was to be explained in occupational terms. As indicated
below, however, Catholics and Protestants do not differ
significantly in terms of occupation.

Comparison of Protestants and Catholics in terms of
occupational status.

Religion	Prof.	Wh. Col.	Skld Lab.	Unskld Lab.
Cath. (n = 164)	17.1%	36.0%	26.8%	20.1%
Prot. (n = 88)	17.0	35.2	23.9	23.9

x^2 = .58 NS 3df

As the table indicates, slight differences exist between Catholics and Protestants in terms of occupational
status. These are clearly insignificant. Therefore, it
seems that the unique religious group in occupational
terms is the Jewish one. A socioeconomic explanation of
some peculiar voting habit might have meaning if Jewish
voters were those exhibiting this peculiar trait and
Protestants and Catholics were most alike. However, this
is not the case. Rather, Jews and Protestants have been
found to be most alike and Catholics unique. Therefore,

an explanation of this difference in socioeconomic terms
is suspect, despite the fact that significant differences
have been found to exist between Catholics, Protestants,
and Jews.

It has so far been indicated that explanations of
the present findings regarding the importance of racial
attitude to the Catholic vote in terms of socioeconomic
status, intensity of religious identification, or partisan intensity are unsatisfactory. In each instance,
Catholics have been indicated to be either not significantly different from non-Catholics or significantly different but not in the suggested manner. Perhaps a temporal explanation will do.

It may be that the present findings are time-bound
to the 1972 election. Perhaps Catholics are normally no
different from non-Catholics in electoral terms except
that the overwhelming popularity of Richard Nixon caused
them to be somewhat more selective in 1972. In future
elections where such a popular candidate will be absent
from the ballot, perhaps the racial issue will mean no
more to Catholics than to other voters. This hypothesis
may be suggested from some of the data. For this purpose, it may be edifying to review the data regarding the
relationship between religion and party affiliation, shown
previously in Chapter 4. The following table does this.

Religion	Republican	Democrat
Prot. (n = 78)	51.3%	48.7%
Cath. (n = 149)	46.3	53.7
Jew. (n = 178)	22.5	77.5

$$x^2 = 28.54 \qquad P = .001 \; 2df \qquad C = .2566$$

As the data indicate, a majority of Catholics consider themselves Democrats. Nevertheless, for the five
1972 elections being studied, the M.D.V. for Catholic respondents was 42.1 percent. Evidently, a considerable
number of Catholic respondents either switched parties
for the 1972 election or split their ballot. This is
also the case even when the great popularity of the Nixon
candidacy is removed from the analysis. Although Mr.
Nixon was very successful among Catholic respondents, the
M.D.V. for the other four elections is only 45.6 percent,
some 8 percent lower than the number of Catholics who
consider themselves Democrats. It may be suggested that
the unique behavior of the Catholic voters is a function
of this Republican electoral success in very short terms
only. With the removal of this unusual variable--that is,

in following elections--perhaps race will not be so important to the Catholic voter.

However, it should also be noted that there were many non-Catholic Democrats who were also affected by the Nixon candidacy. As the table above shows, a large majority of Jewish respondents indicated their preference for the Democratic party (77.5 percent). Nevertheless, the M.D.V. for Jewish respondents in these five elections was only 63.1 percent. Similarly, 48.7 percent of the Protestant respondents considered themselves Democrats, while the M.D.V. for that group was only 45 percent. It is evident that the popularity of the Republican candidate had an impact upon voters of all three religious groups. To explain the unique nature of the Catholic vote largely in terms of the 1972 presidential landslide would therefore seem unsatisfactory.

In addition, to argue that the present data and the apparent importance of racial attitude to the Catholic voter are time-bound to 1972 in fact begs the question. Even assuming that the findings are time-bound, and that they can be defined as a function of short-term factors, does not explain why these factors influenced the Catholic vote alone. It has already been demonstrated that socioeconomic, partisan, or religious factors probably do not play a major role in these findings. It should be expected that the Nixon candidacy would affect all respondents equally. What is there in the Catholic vote that makes it more susceptible to such short-term influences? What was there in the 1972 election that should emphasize the importance of race to the Catholic voter alone? The proposed explanation deals with neither of these issues. Coupled with the above findings regarding the general tendencies of all respondents, the time-bound hypothesis falls far short of meaningfully explaining the unique nature of the Catholic vote.

Yet another possible explanation may help in understanding the present data. Until now, religious groups have been compared to each other without much consideration for the possible further ethnic division of the groups in question. However, the present study allows for national as well as religious designation of Catholics, the very group of interest here. While nationality has not been emphasized because it was found not to be significantly related to most of the political variables herein being tested, it is not unreasonable to assume that nationality will play a role in a finding unique to Catholics.

It has been pointed out, here and elsewhere, that in the area of race relations especially, nationality differences exist within the Catholic community. Of the three main Catholic nationality groups being here dealt with-- Irish, Italian, and German--many sources indicate Italians to be most negatively disposed to integration and civil rights programs.[10] In addition, the generally weaker ties of Italian Catholics to the Democratic party have also been noted.[11] This greater concern with race and weaker commitment to the Democratic party may be significant in the present study. This is particularly true because the majority of Catholics in the present sample are Italian.

The relative importance of the Italian contingent within the Catholic sample can easily be tested in terms of the importance of racial attitude vis-á-vis the vote. This may be accomplished by relating racial attitude to the vote controlling for nationality among Catholic respondents. If the peculiar finding is due to the influence of Italian respondents, it may be expected that racial attitude will remain significant in relation to the vote only among Italians, while it will no longer be significant for the Irish-German group. If, however, racial attitude remains significant for both categories of Catholics, or becomes generally insignificant for Italians or both categories, it would suggest that the pronounced importance of racial attitude is not peculiar to Italians alone. Rather, it would imply that the importance of racial attitude in voting is either a characteristic of each Catholic nationality group or a trait which surfaces only when all Catholics are studied and is therefore characteristic of Catholics as a religious group, depending upon the finding. The following table tests this.

Relationship between racial attitude and the vote, when nationality is held constant for Catholics, 2df.

Election	Italians		Irish-German	
	x^2	c	x^2	c
Pres.	6.78	.3011	8.15	.3619
Cong.	7.35	.3145	1.79 - NS	-
State Sen.	4.08 - NS	-	4.30 - NS	-
C'ty Sher.	7.10	.3095	0.28 - NS	-
T'n Just.	1.77 - NS	-	0.08 - NS	-

(Italians have been compared to Germans and Irish as a group for both substantive and methodological purposes. The present hypothesis argues that it is the predominance of Italians in the Catholic sample which is

126

influencing the findings. It is therefore important to
test these same findings when Italians are removed.
Secondly, because of the large group of Italians in the
sample, the joining of Irish and German is necessary in
order to have sufficiently large distributions to perform
the chi-square test.)

As indicated, the presence of large numbers of Italians in the sample is not sufficient to explain the importance of racial attitude to the Catholic voter. In
the first instance, racial attitude remains quite significant to the German-Irish group at the presidential level.
In fact, judging from the value of C in the presidential
election, racial attitude is a stronger variable among
Irish and German Catholics than among Italians. Secondly,
in two of the five elections, the relationship between
racial attitude and the vote becomes insignificant among
Italian respondents. It appears that racial attitude is
a consistently significant variable only to Catholic voters as a group. However, when the group is further divided by nationality, many of the relationships lose their
significance. Something seems unique to the Catholic
voter, rather than to a particular nationality group of
Catholic voters, which results in the pronounced importance of racial attitude in relation to the vote. Nevertheless, it may be noted that racial attitude is somewhat
more significant to the Italian voter--with the possible
exception of the presidential election--than to the Irish
or German voter, for whom nationality intervened in the
relationship between racial attitude and the vote four of
five times.

One final attempt at explanation will be made. Until
now the explanatory emphasis has related to the vote primarily, and attempts have been made to interpret the findings by studying present socioeconomic, political, national, or psychological differences among the respondents.
It is possible that the key may be more historical. Perhaps something may be gained by analyzing the historical
genesis of the affiliations of the various groups to their
parties.

Essentially, two relevant models of an ethnic group's
affiliation have been forwarded. The first--referred to
as the sociohistorical model--argues that a group's attachment to a particular party may well be the result of
some past historical experience in which a party attempted
to attract the group and the group actively aligned with
the party. Such an event may be viewed as a "critical
election."[12] Such an election is one in which the group--

in this instance an ethnic group--first became involved
in nonlocal politics and was identified with a major party.
This identification is likely to linger for many years,
perhaps long after it has lost its apparent usefulness.
For example, many ethnic groups may be linked with the
Democratic party because of the importance of the urban
party machines during the immigration period. Similarly,
the "New Deal" coalition, forged in the midst of the depression, maintained itself far beyond the thirties.

Conversely, it has been asserted that partisan identification is more rational than sociohistorical. This
model may be termed the rational-historical model. It
argues that there are definite rational and consistent
functions for a group's partisan affiliations, and these
are the significant elements in determining the vote.
Therefore, if an electoral coalition is maintained, it is
less a "political culture lag" than a rational alignment
of groups.[13]

Without determining the merits of this controversy,
it is possible to apply it to the present data. Perhaps
what has been found is a qualitative difference between
the party affiliation of the Protestant-Jewish voters and
that of the Catholic voters. It may be that the ties
felt between Protestants and Jews and their parties are
largely social. Therefore, the particular racial positions of the group members do not play so much of a role
in electoral decision, for the elements that define the
vote are more social than ideological.

Not so with Catholics, however. Perhaps ideological
variables, particularly those relating to race, intervene
here in causing the vote. This may be due to the fact
that for Catholics the partisan affiliation is more ideological than social, and it would be naturally expected
that such attitudinal elements would gain significance.

Further historical analysis may offer greater sophistication to this hypothesis. Should it be determined that
the Catholic party tie is more ideological, while the
Jewish-Protestant tie is more social, this may denote differing partisan experiences. Perhaps the Catholic tie is
more bound to the period of immigration, when the large
urban machines were often connected with the Catholic--
especially Irish--poor. Since this tie is quite old, it
may have outlived even its social impact for younger
Catholics and given way to a more rational-ideological
partisan affiliation in which racial attitude plays a
more significant role than ancient "critical elections."

The Protestant-Jewish model may have had less to do with the immigrant period. This may be the case for Protestants especially, who had little experience with this form of urban life. Perhaps the Protestant-Jewish tie to their party is more bound to the period of the New Deal. The more recent nature of such a tie, and the possibly greater relevance of this era, may result in a party commitment in which ideological elements will play a more limited role.

An immediate qualification may be added, however. Because the data so far have indicated a distinctive quality in the Catholic vote, the Protestant and Jewish respondents have been dealt with as a group. In this hypothesis, this may not be applicable. While the immigrant experience may not play a role in the Protestant vote, it may well play a role in the Jewish vote. Indeed, it should be recalled that the relationship between racial attitude and the vote holding religion constant (the basis of this entire discussion) was somewhat stronger among Jews than among Protestants (see page 114). This may be of significance in this analysis, implying that while the Catholic vote is unique, Jews are somewhat more like Catholics than are Protestants.

If this hypothesis is correct, it might be expected that because of the postulated ideological nature of the Catholic vote, the relationship between racial attitude and party affiliation will be direct and significant. For Jews and Protestants, it may be expected that social elements--in this instance religion--will intervene in the relationship between racial attitude and party affiliation. This will imply that ideological elements are not as important in this relationship as they are for Catholics. It may be, however, that Jews will be closer to Catholics than will Protestants. This is due to the immigrant influence in their partisan commitment which, because of its hypothesized demise and decay, permits the greater influence of ideological elements. Therefore, it may not be surprising to find a direct relationship between racial attitude and party affiliation among Jews which is weaker than among Catholics. The following tests this.

Relationship between racial attitude and party affiliation when religion is held constant, 2df.

Protestants		Catholics		Jews	
x^2	C	x^2	C	x^2	C
3.18 - NS	-	18.07	.3301	9.64	.2278

As the table indicates, no direct relationship exists between racial attitude and party affiliation for Protestants. For Catholics, however, there is a strong relationship which, aside from being significant, also yields a C value higher than that of the simple relationship between racial attitude and party for all respondents (.2756--see page 115). For Jews, the relationship remained significant. Nevertheless, it should be noted that the C value for Jewish respondents (.2278) is lower than that of Catholic respondents (.3301), as well as that of the simple relationship between racial attitude and party affiliation (.2756). It seems that for Protestants, party affiliation--which it must be recalled has been found to be the primary element in relation to the vote--is not directly related to racial attitude. This suggests the more sociohistorical nature of the Protestant partisan commitment. For Catholics, and to a lesser extent for Jews, it appears that the relationship between party affiliation and racial attitude is direct. Perhaps this implies a more ideological and rational tie to partisan affiliations. This may help explain the unique nature of the Catholic vote and may suggest that the Jewish vote is next to be affected by these same ideological elements in relation to their partisan affiliation.

CAUSALITY: A SUMMARY ANALYSIS

To accommodate the findings relative to data outlined in previous chapters, a causal model of the vote has been attempted. It was found that party affiliation, racial attitude, and religious identification are the three most significant variables in relation to the vote. Based upon the magnitude of the C values, it was hypothesized that party affiliation would be most directly related to the vote, with racial attitude and religion following in that order.

This model was tested by means of control data with the qualification that the statistical tests used indicate association rather than causation and do not discriminate between spurious and intervening relationships. The nature of the results did permit the suggestion that findings were not spurious but rather implied indirect causal paths when significance levels dropped under controlled conditions.

It was confirmed, on the basis of a series of such tests, that the strongest and most consistently direct relationship existed between party affiliation and the vote. Neither religion nor racial attitude intervened in this relationship.

However, when party affiliation was held constant, it was generally found that religion did not consistently relate significantly with the vote. Similarly, racial attitude was generally insignificant in relation to the vote when party was held constant. A weak and inconsistent relationship did persist between religion and the vote, and racial attitude and the vote, even with party held constant. This was incorporated in the causal model.

The findings became more complex when racial attitude was related to the vote, holding religion constant, as well as when religion was related to the vote, controlling for racial attitude. When the second test was done, it was generally found that religion did not relate consistently with the vote to a significant degree. This suggested the intervening nature of racial attitude in the relationship between religion and the vote. The weak relationship that did persist between religion and the vote under such controlled conditions was also added to the model.

However, when racial attitude was related to the vote, holding religion constant, it was found that while for Protestants and Jews the relationship was not consistently significant, for Catholics the relationship actually increased (judging from the magnitude of the C value). This seemed to suggest that for Catholics racial attitude plays a greater role in determining the vote than for Protestants and Jews. Based upon this finding it was decided that two models would be needed. One of these would accommodate the unique nature of the Catholic vote, while the second would trace the vote of Jews and Protestants.

Attempts were then made to explain this interesting finding. Hypotheses regarding the intensity of religious identification and partisan affiliation were analyzed. It was found that Catholics do not differ in the expected directions from non-Catholics, suggesting that such hypotheses would not satisfactorily explain the data.

Similar tests were attempted to ascertain the role of socioeconomic status. It was found that Catholics do not differ significantly from non-Catholics in terms of education, although they do in terms of occupational status. Further investigation indicated, however, that Catholics and Protestants do not differ significantly in terms of occupation, although Jews do differ from both.

This suggested that were there to be a unique group, it should be expected that such designation would fall to Jewish respondents. Occupational differences could not sufficiently explain the unique nature of the Catholic vote, however. On this basis, the socioeconomic hypothesis was not accepted.

A temporal explanation was then extended. It was hypothesized that the present data were time-bound to the 1972 election. The absence of a landslide Republican victory in the future, however, would render the Catholic vote no different from that of non-Catholics. Such an explanation could not be fully acceptable, it was pointed out. While it may limit the scope of the findings, it in fact merely begged the question. Even assuming that the hypothesis was correct, it was still unclear why Catholics should be so affected by the Nixon candidacy while others were not. It was further noted that all three religious groups were affected by the Republican presidential victory of 1972. A temporal hypothesis would not therefore be sufficient to explain the unique strength of racial attitude as a variable in relation to the Catholic vote.

A further ethnic breakdown was then attempted. It was reasoned that the large contingent of Italians in the Catholic sample may be influencing the data. It was noted that other studies had found a greater sensitivity on the part of Italian Catholics to questions of race as well as a lesser commitment to the Democratic party. The results of testing for this relationship yielded generally negative findings, however. It was found that when Italians alone were tested for racial attitude in relation to the vote, the previously significant relationship became insignificant in three of five cases. In addition, at the presidential level the German-Irish category yielded a stronger relationship between racial attitude and the vote than did the Italian. The generally greater importance of racial attitude to the Italian Catholic than to the German or Irish was noted, however.

A final, sociohistorical hypothesis was then raised. It was postulated that a qualitative difference existed between the party affiliations of the Catholic respondents and those of the Jews and Protestants. This was explained in historical terms. It was suggested that the Catholic commitment to the Democratic party was largely rooted in the immigrant experience, one which may not be relevant any longer. It is not unreasonable to assume, therefore, that ideological elements--racial attitude, for instance--

would be of greater significance to the less sentimentally committed Catholic voter. Perhaps because of the more recent nature of the Protestant-Jewish affiliation, dating to the New Deal, this would not be true of these two groups. They might still be affected by the "critical elections" of the thirties, in which strong and maintaining coalitions were forged. In addition, the Protestants experienced little of the immigrants' need for the urban machine. This indicates an immediate difference between the quality of the Catholic and Protestant party affiliations.

In order to test this hypothesis, the nature of the relationship between racial attitude and party was explored. It was found that for Catholics, racial attitude was directly related to party affiliation, which implies the rational nature of their partisan commitment. For Protestants this was not found to be the case, thus indicating the more sociohistorical nature of their party affiliation. For Jews, however, a direct and significant relationship between racial attitude and party affiliation was found, contrary to expectations. It was hypothesized that because the Jewish partisan commitment may also be grounded in the immigrant experience, it may be expected that they will be more similar to Catholics than are Protestants. The lower C value found in the Jewish case did partially confirm the hypothesis, which implies that racial attitude was most directly related to partisan affiliation in the case of the Catholic voter.

Nevertheless, the hypothesis is far from confirmed. Aside from the implications of these hypotheses, little else can be said about the peculiar nature of the Catholic respondents. In fact, most attempts at explanation here have resulted in negative conclusions. Even those partially confirmed, such as the role of the Italian respondents or the qualitative partisan affiliation of the groups, are far from satisfactory explanations. However, they are as much as the present data permit and at least partially explain the two causal models of suburban voting behavior herein presented.

NOTES

1. Much of the ensuing discussion, as well as the model for the causal diagrams used, was adapted from the following sources: H. M. Blalock, Social Statistics (New York: McGraw-Hill, 1960), especially pp. 337-43; W. Miller and D. Stokes, "Constituency Influence in Congress," in

A. Campbell et al., ed., <u>Elections and the Political Order</u>
(New York: J. Wiley, 1966), chap. 16; H. Simon, "Spurious
Correlation: A Causal Interpretation," in H. M. Blalock,
ed., <u>Causal Models in the Social Sciences</u> (Chicago: Aldine-
Atherton, 1971), chap. 1; A. Goldberg, "Discerning a
Causal Pattern Among Data on Voting Behavior," in Blalock,
ed., <u>Causal Models in the Social Sciences</u>, op. cit., chap.
3.

2. Simon, op. cit., p. 9.

3. See Simon, op. cit., p. 16; also Blalock, <u>Social
Statistics</u>, op. cit., p. 339.

4. The basis for this procedure and the following
set of tables is Goldberg, op. cit., especially pp. 37-46.

5. E. Banfield and J. Wilson, <u>City Politics</u> (Cambridge: Harvard University and M.I.T., 1963); also, same
authors, "Public-Regardedness as a Value-Premise for Voting
Behavior," <u>American Political Science Review</u> (December
1964): 876-87; also, same authors, "Political Ethos Revisited," same <u>Review</u> (December 1971): 1048-62.

6. A. Campbell, <u>White Attitudes Toward Black People</u>
(Ann Arbor: University of Michigan, 1971), pp. 46-49.

7. A. Greely, <u>Why Can't They Be Like Us</u> (New York:
E. P. Dutton, 1971), chap. 6.

8. E. Wakin and J. Scheuer, <u>The DeRomanization of
the American Catholic Church</u> (New York: Macmillan, 1966),
chaps. 11 and 13.

9. D. P. Moynihan and N. Glazer, <u>Beyond the Melting
Pot</u> (Cambridge: Harvard University and M.I.T., 1970),
p. xxvi.

10. Greely, op. cit.

11. Ibid.; also M. Levey and M. Kramer, <u>The Ethnic
Factor</u> (New York: Simon & Schuster, 1972), chap. 7.

12. For a full development of this thesis in reference to ethnic groups, see R. Wolfinger, "The Development
and Persistence of Ethnic Voting," <u>American Political
Science Review</u> (December 1965): 896-908.

13. For the most recent statement of this postulation, with empirical evidence to support it, see D.
Repass, "Issue Salience and Party Choice," <u>American Political Science Review</u> (June 1971): 389-400.

7

ETHNICITY, POLITICS, AND SUBURBIA: CONCLUSIONS

The subject of the present study has been the influence of ethnicity upon suburban political behavior. The
data were taken from a survey administered in the town
of Ramapo, in New York State, in the spring of 1973. It
was divided into three main areas: voting behavior, political attitudes, and interest-participation levels.
In each area, the influence of ethnicity was statistically
tested and compared to the impact of several other variables. In addition, some attempt has been made at con-
structing a causal model inferred from the data utilizing
those variables which have proven to be most significant.
It remains yet to summarize the findings and conclude
with some comments and suggestions for future research.

THE CONTEXT AND HYPOTHESES

The motivation for this study came from two sources.
The author was struck simultaneously with the paucity of
systematic theories regarding suburban voting and political culture, and the relative nonexistence of ethnicity
as a political variable in the literature regarding suburbia. It was evident that a major contribution could be
made by furthering the frontiers of research in both the
areas of suburban politics and ethnic politics. Indeed,
how much greater the significance if ethnicity could be
suggested as the major variable in suburban political
culture.

The prior studies did not preclude such a finding.
Suburbanites have been characterized as converts (to
either Republicanism and/or frenetic but irrelevant political detail), as well as transformers of culture who

bring their values, attitudes, and political orientations with them. Various impressionistic and empirical studies have concluded that partisanship is irrelevant in the suburbs, that suburbanites are Republicans, that the values of community and uniformity predominate, and that suburbia has no real political culture. Indeed, each succeeding study tests and modifies the conclusions of its predecessors and sometimes results in contradictory and confusing results. Nevertheless, little has previously been said about the possible role of ethnicity in the suburban political arena.

Indeed, there seems reason to believe that ethnicity might well be a significant factor in suburban politics. No matter whether a new suburban resident changes his political affiliations or attitudes in fact, it is still likely that he will be somewhat affected by his new address. Prior studies have suggested that suburbia will be a region of little political culture and "no party politics," that the change to suburban living will result in a weakening of previous political ties and partisan affiliations.[1] Thus, while the theory that suburban residence automatically implies Republican affiliation may have been largely contradicted by the results of the 1960 election, it was still possible that the affinity to the party of previous affiliation--indeed to any party at all--may have been weakened by the suburban move. Perhaps ethnicity might fill the vacuum created in the mind of the voter because of the suburban move. It was thought that rather than take his cues from party affiliation, social class, candidate perceptions, or any of the other variables normally studied in connection with voting habits, ethnicity might serve this function.

Ethnicity was chosen to fulfill this need for several reasons. It was first noted that some previous sociological studies have indicated the existence in suburban areas of ethnic enclaves similar to those found in many cities. This seemed to imply that ethnics might seek each other out--as like-minded, suitable neighbors. Indeed, studies indicated the high level of participation in religious and cultural activities among suburban residents. It was further reasoned that the forces of community and uniformity, strongly enforced in suburban society, might encourage such religious participation and identification, albeit for other than theological reasons. Such elements could not help but have an impact upon the electoral and attitudinal orientations of the suburban resident.[2]

Ethnicity was also chosen as a likely influence in suburban politics because it has greater visibility than most other of the variables. In order for issues to be politically salient, for example, it is necessary that they exist, that voters recognize their existence, and that voters deem them relevant to their own needs, and that candidates or parties present clear and meaningful alternatives to the voters so that they may act upon their issue perceptions. Because of the complexity of such a variable, and its requirements in terms of interest and participation, it was hypothesized that ethnicity would be more important.

This is also the case with social class. In order for this to be a relevant variable, it is necessary that the voter recognize his own social class and its political implications. In addition, he must have some meaningful electoral choice and recognize it in terms of either party or candidates. This too was not considered very likely.

Therefore, because the ethnic identity of a candidate is often recognizable from his name, it was reasoned that ethnicity would have greater impact than other variables. Further, though party affiliation is also recognizable on the ballot, it was reasoned that its influence would be weakened as a result of the impact of the suburban move. It was argued that suburbanites would vote for candidates of their own ethnic group membership.

In addition, it was clearly recognized that ethnicity might have a second impact upon the vote. Aside from the influence of the candidate's ethnic identification, it may be that the voter's own ethnic identifications might influence his perceptions and values. This would manifest itself in a more subtle manner. It would mean that voters of similar ethnic identity would vote similarly. Such a hypothesis would also have obvious implications in terms of attitudes and political participation. If voters of the same ethnic group tend to vote alike, it is not unreasonable to assume that they also may have similar interest levels in the political arena. It was therefore further hypothesized that ethnicity would be more significant in relation to the dependent variables of political attitudes and interest participation than such factors as party affiliation, social class, candidate perceptions, and so forth.

In order to test these speculations regarding the voting habits, political attitudes, and interest of suburbanites in the context of their ethnic identifications,

a random sampling of 519 suburban voters was drawn. Names
were chosen from the registration rolls of the town of
Ramapo, some 30 miles north of New York City. Voters were
asked a series of personal questions regarding their education, occupation, party affiliation, ethnicity attitudes,
political participation, and interest levels. They were
also asked to indicate their choices for various electoral
races on a re-creation of the 1972 ballot, as well as a
proposed ballot for 1973. This method allowed the author
to compare the influence of ethnicity upon suburban politics with the influences from the voters' party affiliation, occupation, education, interests, and so forth. It
would allow an empirical test of whether ethnicity would
be the most important variable in relation to the voting
habits, attitudes, and interest-participation levels of
the suburban voter, as hypothesized.

THE DATA

By and large, the hypotheses were not confirmed. In
terms of voting, it was found that though ethnicity had
been defined as religion as well as nationality for Catholics, only religion related significantly to the vote. In
addition, this relationship was apparent only insofar as
members of the same ethnic group tended to vote similarly.
Voters were not found to vote to any significant degree
for candidates of their own ethnic group.

Further, in reviewing the voting data, it was found
that the apparent relationship between religion and the
vote was weaker (as noted by the comparative magnitude of
the C value) than the relationships found between both
party affiliation and the vote and the subject's attitude
toward residential integration and the vote. It seemed
that these two latter variables--party affiliation and
attitude toward residential integration--were more strongly related to the vote than was religion. The three, however, were far more important (both in terms of the relative strength of the C value and the consistency of significant relationships) than occupation, education, other
attitudes (such as those on drug abuse, law and order,
welfare, or educational spending), interest, participation, or candidate and party perception. Evidently, these
three variables were well worth further examination in
the hope that some meaningful causal model might be inferred from them.

138

Much the same was found to be true when the subject's political attitudes were analyzed. The data did not confirm ethnicity as the most important variable in relation to the voter's political attitudes. In fact, in many instances ethnicity was not at all significantly related to the particular attitude. This was true in the case of educational spending, trust in local government, and the building of high-rise apartments. In these issue-areas, socioeconomic considerations appeared to be paramount, and education and occupation surfaced as the most strongly related variables. Interestingly, party affiliation also did not relate significantly to any of these issues. It was suggested that these issues may have been somewhat removed from the electoral setting; thus those very factors which were related to the vote most significantly--party affiliation and religion--were not important here.

However, in other issue-areas, notably law and order, drug abuse, and welfare, party affiliation and religion took on preeminent importance. In these areas it was evident that the voter's attitudes, partisan preferences, and his religious identifications were significantly related. Most interesting, because of its prior relationship with the vote, was the residential segregation issue. Here, both party affiliation and religion related strongly. Evidently, not only was there a relationship between these three variables and the vote, but a significant relationship also existed among the variables themselves. This largely eliminated the possibility that some or all of these variables operated independently in relation to the vote. It also opened several intriguing possibilities relating to the creation of a causal model of the influence of ethnicity upon the suburban vote.

It should finally be noted that as with the data on voting habits, no significant relationship was found to exist between attitudes and nationality for Catholic respondents. Generally, attitudes crossed nationality lines among Catholics, and only strongly qualified comments regarding some noted differences could be made. It seems that to the extent that ethnicity has any impact upon suburban politics at all, it is not defined by nationality, for Catholics, in the present data.

The third area of suburban politics under discussion regards the voter's interests and participation levels. Respondents were asked to indicate the frequency with which they discussed local politics, read the local newspaper, listened to the local radio stations, and so forth. In addition, they were asked to approximate their own interest in local politics and whether they had voted in the 1972 election. Of all three dependent variables, voting, attitudes, and interest-participation, ethnicity was found to be least important here. By and large, respondents were found to participate and to involve themselves actively in local affairs, or so they claimed. This interest and participation crossed ethnic lines, as well as crossing most other categories--such as socioeconomic, partisan, and attitudinal.

In general, the only variable which did relate significantly to tests of interest and participation were occupation and intensity of partisan affiliation. It was found that a positive relationship existed between intensity of partisan affiliation and interest. For instance, those whose partisan affiliations were strongest tended to be more interested in local affairs and claimed to participate more regularly than those whose partisan affiliations were weaker. A similarly positive relationship was also found to exist when occupational status was related to tests of political interest-participation, the results indicated that those with higher occupational status (professionals and white-collar workers) claimed higher degrees of interest than those of lower status. Other than these two variables, it appeared that the claim to participation and interest in local affairs crossed ethnic, party, and attitudinal lines and did not generally relate to any variable in a regular and systematic fashion.

Before leaving this area of political interest, one more note is in order. It has been found that political interest and participation as a dependent variable acted largely independently of the various factors being tested. Rather than dividing along given lines such as socioeconomic and attitudinal, respondents seemed to claim, almost universally, high levels of interest by almost every test. While it is not unlikely that such findings reflect the actual situations (the reader is reminded that prior students of suburbia have found a high level of political interest and participation, see Chapter 5), it is equally likely that subjects did not respond quite candidly to interviewers in this area. Undoubtedly, such criticism may also be leveled at each section of the present study. However, the almost universal nature of the participation levels makes the data somewhat more suspect.

In addition, it may well be that the testing for political interest requires techniques more sophisticated than those used here. The temptation to inflate one's participation or interest in a suburban area which may

well value "civic virtue and local participation" may have
been too great to be overcome by the questions used in the
present study. Further, respondents may have been unable--
or unwilling--to differentiate between reading or listening
to local news "several times a week, once a week . . .
etc." or between actually reading the local section of the
local paper and simply owning the paper. A more definitive
means of checking the veracity of responses and further
testing a subject's interest may be necessary before the
conclusion that suburbanites have a very high level of political interest-participation may be reached. Also, similar sophisticated techniques must be used in further
studies before it can be concluded that ethnicity plays
virtually no role in suburban interest-participation levels. Until then, however, the present data will have to
be accepted at face value.

If our base is these three substantive chapters dealing with the simple relationships between several sociopolitical variables and the three dependent ones--voting,
attitudes, and interest--it must be said that the earlier
hypotheses regarding the primary impact of ethnicity upon
suburban politics must be severely modified at best and
entirely abandoned in certain instances. Particularly in
the area of interest, ethnicity--by any definition--proved
to be largely insignificant as a variable. Indeed, this
was the case with many variables; it may be as much due to
lack of candor on the part of respondents as to the actual
absence of statistical relationships, as noted above.

In terms of attitudes as well, ethnicity--defined as
nationality--for Catholics was not found to relate significantly to the respondents' attitudes regarding major
local issue-areas.

Only in the area of voting did ethnicity--defined
only as religion--prove to be of some consistent significance. Here it was found that contrary to the hypothesis,
nationality did not relate significantly to the vote of
Catholic respondents, and ethnics did not generally vote
for fellow-ethnic candidates. However, members of the
same religious group did tend to vote similarly. This
relationship, however, did not prove to be stronger than
that found to exist between party affiliation (far and
away the strongest single variable) and the respondent's
attitude regarding residential segregation.

Based upon these modifications and reorientations in
the original hypotheses, a causal model was attempted.
This model was presented schematically as a progression
toward the vote, which served as the dependent variable.

Several relationships were tested under controlled circumstances and the chi-square test of significance was used to determine whether any given variable intervened between another and the vote. (In the schematic presentations, the discovery that a particular controlled test yielded an insignificant result was held to be comparable to the zero correlation finding of a path analysis. This is not meant to imply that what has been done is anything more than a graphic illustration of the data. Rather, the intention is largely descriptive.)

A number of possible causal relationships were tested by using the three variables found to be most strongly related to the vote: party affiliation, racial attitude, and religion. These involved the sequence of the variables in the progression toward the vote.

Several interesting conclusions emerged. It was found that the relationship between party affiliation and the vote was direct and not affected by controlled experimentation. When both racial attitude--the respondent's attitude toward residential segregation--or religion was held constant, there was little if any impact upon the relationship between party affiliation and the vote.

Such was not the case for the relationships between religion and the vote, or between racial attitude and the vote. Both religion and racial attitude became generally insignificant in relation to the vote when party affiliation was held constant. Further, the relationship between religion and the vote became largely insignificant when racial attitude was held constant.

These four findings permitted the creation of much of a causal model of the present voting data. The missing data regard the relationship between racial attitude and the vote when religion is held constant. In this small area, a very notable finding emerged. It was apparent that for Jews and Protestants the relationship between racial attitude and the vote became insignificant in five of ten possible instances. However, for Catholics the relationship between racial attitude and the vote remained significant at all levels. This was taken to imply the unusual tenacity of the Catholic respondent's racial attitude in relation to that of his Protestant and Jewish suburban neighbors. To account for this final result in the context of the four outlined above, two models were constructed. These are presented below in Figures 7.1 and 7.2.

FIGURE 7.1

The Protestant and Jewish Vote

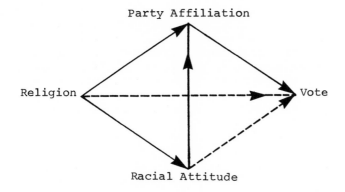

FIGURE 7.2

The Catholic Vote

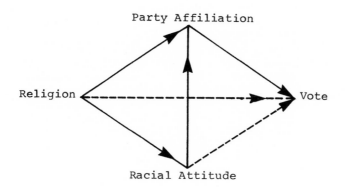

Once again, the reader is reminded that unbroken lines signify consistently direct relationships, while broken lines signify relationships that are not consistently direct. For the Jewish and Protestant voter it seems that party affiliation carries on a direct relationship with the vote and intervenes in the relationship between the other two variables and the vote. In addition, in this model it was found that the relationship between religion and the vote becomes insignificant in most cases when racial attitude is held in control. Similarly, racial attitude becomes insignificant in five of ten instances when related to the vote holding religion constant. This mutually intervening relationship has been represented in the diagram by means of two-headed arrows.

In the Catholic model, the sequence and progression toward the vote is largely the same. Party affiliation is still the variable most directly related to the vote. The relationship between religion and the vote becomes insignificant in most instances when party or racial attitude is held constant. Finally, the relationship between racial attitude and the vote becomes insignificant when party affiliation is held constant, in most instances. The only difference between the two models lies in the fact that the two-headed arrows connecting racial attitude and religion found in the Protestant-Jewish model and implying a mutually intervening relationship with the vote are absent in the Catholic model. The relationship between racial attitude and the vote is at no time affected by religion and never becomes insignificant when religion is held in control. In fact, judging by the strength of the C values, the relationship between racial attitude and the vote actually increases in strength for Catholics in four of five cases.

Finally, attempts were made to explain the unique nature of the Catholic vote. Sociological explanations based upon socioeconomic differences of Catholic voters, or the degree of their religious identification, were tested and found inadequate. Political explanations based upon the relative degree of partisan affiliation and the temporal context of the elections in question were also tested and rejected. Two final possibilities were tested and partially accepted to explain the findings.

It was postulated that the data for Catholic voters might be influenced by the large Italian representation among Catholic respondents. It is possible that what had been assumed to be characteristic of Catholics generally was in fact characteristic of Italian Catholics specifically. This hypothesis was partially confirmed. When nationality was held in control, and the relationship between racial attitude and the vote was tested for Catholics, the results were not significant for non-Italians in four of five instances but remained significant for Italians in three of five. Therefore, it appeared that Italians were more sensitive to the issue of race in their electoral choices than were non-Italian Catholics. Nevertheless, this could only serve as a partial explanation. The circumstances under which racial attitude and the vote relate significantly in all five cases are apparently present only when Catholics as a whole are studied rather than when a particular nationality group is tested. (The findings indicate one of the peculiarities of the chi-square statistic. When a relationship is found to exist even when controls are applied, like the one between racial attitude and the vote for Catholics, it is still dangerous to make inferences regarding the data, for it is possible that other variables are intricately involved in the relationship. Thus when nationality is held constant, the relationship between racial attitude and the vote for Catholics becomes weaker and less consistent.)

It was also suggested that the difference between the two models may well be based upon qualitative differences in their respective partisan ties. Two models of party affiliation were forwarded. The first is the social model in which critical elections determine party affiliations for many years to come—even after the events which led to the group's support of a particular party are absent. The second is the rational model in which party affiliation is the result of the well-defined needs of the group and the function that the party may perform at a given time.

This dichotomy was superimposed upon the findings, and it was suggested that the Catholic ties to the Democratic party—linked as they were to the urban machines and the immigrant era—no longer served a purpose to the present Catholic voter. It is only natural to expect that the very important attitudinal variable of race relations should gain significance. For the Protestant voter whose party affiliations were far less affected by immigration, it was suggested that the party tie was largely the result of the "critical" elections of the New Deal. This more recent and perhaps more social orientation could mean a lesser sensitivity to the racial issue in determining the vote. The Jewish respondent, despite his immigrant experience, may have a sociohistorical orientation toward his party affiliation which is also grounded more in the New Deal experience. Therefore, it may be expected that he will be the next to be affected by the racial issue, although less so than the more "rational-ideological" Catholic voter.

This explanation is obviously tentative. More study must be done to determine the role of religion in the formation of attitudes and party affiliation. At the present time, this latter explanation--in addition to the previous comments regarding the role of nationality in understanding the nature of the Catholic vote--may help explain the present results.

THE FINAL PERSPECTIVE

In order to conclude this study, two more questions have yet to be discussed. The first traces its thrust from the original hypotheses presented in Chapter 1. The second is closely related to the data that actually emerged from the survey.

The first question is: Why were the hypotheses not generally confirmed? By and large, it was found that the role of ethnicity in attitude formation and participation levels is minimal and important in voting only under certain specific conditions, as outlined above. This is quite different from that which was expected, and the considerable disparity from the expected to the observed requires some explanation. Several alternatives come to mind.

The first, and most obvious, is that the hypotheses were simply incorrect. It was assumed that the suburban sociopolitical structure would leave the voter without some simple means of making his choices. It was further assumed that the voter would choose ethnicity to fulfill this need. This simply did not prove correct. If anything, the voter may depend upon partisan affiliation to simplify his choice, although the data suggest a more complicated model. He clearly does not depend upon ethnic identity--by any definition. At best, religion serves as a "background" variable which may influence the direction of the vote. It is hardly the "most important single variable in the suburban political arena" as was earlier postulated. Evidently, the influence of ethnicity was simply miscalculated.

Such an explanation is certainly simple. It may be deceiving in its simplicity, however. It should be recalled that the analysis of data for each political subarea--

voting, attitudes, and interest-participation--was preceded by reviews of the relevant scholarly literature.
At each juncture, it was noted that the work of prior researchers in this area did not preclude, and indeed often
suggested, the possibility that the "ethnic hypothesis"
would be confirmed. To toss aside the hypothesis because
of an assumption based upon the present data would imply
that much of the prior scholarly literature must also be
cast aside. Perhaps this difficulty can be blunted, however, if the aggregate impact of the literature can be
utilized.

It must be recalled that the original hypotheses were
based upon certain premises suggested by prior research.
It was first assumed that partisanship would not be a
major factor in suburban politics, leaving a vacuum in the
voter's political field of vision. It was also assumed
that the suburbanites' political attitudes would be more
socially enforced than party-related (based upon the suburban values of community and social integration in which
ethnicity may play an important role). It was finally
assumed that the level of political interest would be low
and rather sterile or at least inappropriate to the political environment. Each of these premises was based
upon the findings of previous writers, as were the analyses and insights surrounding them.

Therefore, to say that ethnicity was simply not found
to be as salient as hypothesized does not truly explain
the data. Rather, these several premises were unconfirmed.
Partisanship was found to be most important--indicating
that the vacuum assumed to exist in the voter's mind may
not exist at all. Further, suburbanites apparently do
hold politically salient values and attitudes. This is
especially true with regard to the issue of racial integration. In addition, rather than apathy, disinterest,
and sterility, large majorities of respondents claimed
high levels of political participation and exposure to
the local media . . . given the methodological limitation
of the data in this area (see pages 139-40). In effect
it was postulated that ethnicity would replace these several variables in the suburbs. What was found was that
the variables were generally not absent, so that there
was no great vacuum to be filled.

It may also be that the present data do not entirely
preclude the existence of an ethnic suburban influence
similar to the one originally postulated. The present
data have concentrated upon the full spectrum of ethnic
identifiers--from the most intensely identified to the

most apathetic. The data did not permit comprehensive analysis of various subgroups among those of ethnic identity. It may be, however, that within the ethnic groups are those whose identity results in political influence similar to that defined by the original hypothesis.

In order to study such subgroups, however, a more sophisticated methodology than that utilized here would be needed. It would be necessary to study respondents' religious practices, friendship circles, participation in religious-cultural activities, exposure to the means of ethnic-communal communication, and so forth. Therefore, it may be that ethnicity does not have the impact projected for all respondents in the suburban political arena. However, the impact may well exist among certain subgroups within the general ethnic group. This effect may not have been detectable given the methodology used in the present study, which was not designed to differentiate between various forms and intensities of ethnic identification.[3]

It may also be noted that the present study suffers from the general malaise of case studies: exclusivity. It may be argued that what has been presently found in relation to Ramapo is characteristic of Ramapo only. Thus, it may be that in other suburbs in other regions, party affiliation will be of lesser import, and ethnicity will assume the prominence earlier postulated. This comment may be particularly telling due to the partisan nature of Ramapo elections. The present test of ethnic political influence was carried out in a political milieu least likely to fulfill its hypothesis. If ethnicity was to replace partisanship as the significant electoral variable, then such a finding would occur in partisan elections last. The fact that ethnicity did not manifest prominence in Ramapo may therefore imply that its influence is not evident in partisan elections. In other suburban areas, where nonpartisan elections are held, perhaps ethnicity will surface as a variable of greater importance.

Finally, there may be a more comprehensive manner of explaining the fact that the original hypotheses were not confirmed. Perhaps these hypotheses were not so much incorrect as misdirected. The key to understanding the role of ethnicity in suburbia may be in its relation to party affiliation. It is clear that the most pervasive factor influencing the voting habits of the present group of respondents is their party affiliation. This variable has been found to relate most strongly and directly with the vote at every level and under all conditions. It is the author's hypothesis, however, that party affiliation represents not so much one variable as a collection of variables in aggregate. Thus it may be that the party in most cases is the prism within which lights such as those of attitude, socioeconomic status, ethnic identification, and interest levels are refracted and bent into politically relevant responses. This is in fact a variation on the theme of political simplification: the party serves the function of simplifying the voter's choice and helping him to make his values and attitudes more appropriate to the political environment.[4]

Two remarks are in order here. It is first likely that the foregoing definition of the party's function may not hold true for all voters. Doubtless, a hard core of voters are so committed to one or the other party that the party label almost completely subsumes their political responses. Such voters will be found to vote the party ticket no matter who the candidate or what the issues. For the large majority of voters, this is probably not the case. It certainly was not found to be true in the present sample. It was found here that most voters had politically relevant attitudes, and that variables other than party affiliation related to the vote as well as to attitudes and interest levels.

It is also relevant to note that the role that is presently being awarded to the voter's party affiliation was earlier hypothesized to belong to ethnicity. It will be remembered that part of the original hypothesis argued that the proposed increase in the political salience of ethnicity was due to the decrease of the importance of party affiliation in the suburbs. It was projected that, because of the effects of either "conversion" to the suburban value-set or the "transplantation" of changing urban values to the fertile suburban soil, the impact of partisan affiliation would be minimal or at least seriously reduced. Indeed, such were the general findings of Robert Wood in his study of suburban politics.[5] The novelty of the present hypothesis lay in the proposed replacement of this aggregating-simplifying function of the party with that of ethnicity.

What has been found, however, is a form of compromise. Ethnicity has not replaced partisanship. Rather, ethnicity is important to the extent that it relates to partisanship. Precisely because partisanship has been found to be a vital and dynamic influence on the vote, the crucial relationship shifts from that which regards ethnicity and the vote to that which regards ethnicity and partisanship. Clearly, the area for study in a follow-up analysis must be the role of the various factors in relation to party affiliation. Put simply, ethnicity has been found to be somewhat significant--though not at all as significant as first hypothesized. What is important to note here is that to understand the role of ethnicity in suburban politics one must analyze not so much the relationship between it and the vote--which is not a particularly important one--but the relationship between ethnicity and partisanship. Such a direction would be a profitable orientation for future study.

It is recognized that no one of the above explanations fully satisfies the disparity between the hypotheses and the findings. No doubt the answer lay in some combination of all the above. The hypotheses were largely incorrect in that they were based upon premises inferred from the previous literature. These premises did not apply in Ramapo, in 1972. Further, it is still possible that the hypotheses are correct and do apply to certain subdivisions of ethnic groups which were not detected because of the methodology being used in this project. Finally, it is possible that the original postulations were misdirected in that they assumed the influence of ethnicity to be in relation to the vote, while its most important role may be in relation to partisan affiliation. In addition, it is quite possible that there are several other explanations which do not come to mind at present.

Although possible reasons for the nonconfirmation of the original hypothesis have been examined, one question remains to be explored: What are the implications of that which did result? It was generally found that partisan affiliation, attitude toward residential integration, and religious identification were most closely related to the vote. In addition, it was found that the attitude toward racial integration was more important to the Catholic voter than to the Protestant or Jewish voter. It was speculated in explanation that the ties of the Catholic voter to his party may have become politically irrelevant or archaic. For this reason, ideological elements--especially those relating to race--may play a uniquely strong role in influencing the vote.

This finding may imply several future developments. Evidently, the racial question had most electoral impact to the voters in the present sample. Specifically, the issue is one of residential integration on a generally equal basis. The respondents were asked to react to the possibility of Blacks living on their block. Presumably,

the newcomers would be in the same residential circumstances and of the same socioeconomic level. Those issues
in which racial questions were also intermingled with economic, social, or moral questions did not have as potent
an electoral impact. Statements relating to welfare, law
and order, high-rise apartments, or drug abuse had little
consistent electoral impact. Rather, the issue of residential segregation--which was more purely racial--was the
most politically salient.

This finding seems to imply that to a significant
segment of the voting population, socioeconomic elements
are being replaced by ideological ones. Specifically,
these ideological elements are racial and relatively pure
in content. This may seem that the importance of partisanship must be viewed in the context of this change.
Coalitions forged in prior political eras and held together by the momentum of "critical elections" may no
longer be maintained. Indeed, this more social approach
to partisanship may give way to new alignments that could
be projected as future "critical elections."

Specifically, it seems that the Democratic coalitions
based upon the immigrant and New Deal experiences may be
breaking down. While it may have been sufficient to assume that many Catholics would vote Democratic because of
their religious identification and the socioeconomic
status it often implied in former years, the present data
indicate a change. Now it seems evident that though partisanship is quite important to the Catholic voter, it is
partisanship in which the voter's racial ideology plays a
stronger role than might be expected. It is also an
ideology that will have to be taken into account in evalu-
ating the voter's partisanship and, ultimately, his electoral choice as well.

It should be noted that the idea of shifts in the
content and makeup of partisanship in the late sixties
and early seventies is not a novel conception. Burnham
has demonstrated that partisan realignments have taken
place every 35 to 40 years. Specifically, he points to
the elections of 1858 and 1860 as ending one party system
and beginning a second. The new party system continued
until the election of 1896. At this time, territorial
partisanship took precedence and the realignment resulted
in a southern-rural Democratic party and an urban-industrial
G.O.P. This party system continued until the elections of
1930 and 1932 and the depression. It was here that the modern Democratic coalition was first forged. By this cycle
it is to be expected that a new party alignment might develop some 35 to 40 years following the 1932 election,

which would mean the 1972 election, the one presently being studied. Indeed, although Burnham does not fully define the content or nature of the realignments that the cycle dictates, he does project such a development and supports it with empirical data.[6]

Another writer, Kevin Philips, has independently come to similar conclusions and has also conjectured about the form which the partisan realignment will take.[7] It is Philips's thesis that the Democratic coalition built in the New Deal years has outlived its usefulness. Major shifts in the attitudes and values of voters, especially as they relate to race and economic security, will cause a shift in the partisan loyalties of many voters in the direction of the G.O.P. According to Philips, this is especially true in the case of union and Catholic voters who have now entered the middle class and in many instances moved to the suburbs. These voters, Philips claims, are the most susceptible to the appeals of the Republican party and will shift to it in elections immediately to come. To Philips this means the 1972 presidential election.

To some extent, the present data may be used to support the analyses of both Philips and Burnham. Clearly, the voters in the sample under discussion did not move en masse to the Republican party in terms of affiliation, although a large majority of them chose its presidential candidate in 1972. Rather, a majority of them still considered themselves Democrats and did not cross party lines in many of the state or local elections. However, it seems that some of the content of this partisanship may have changed in the directions suggested by Philips and Burnham.

Firstly, the fact that racial attitudes and social issues in coordination with partisanship seem to replace older, more sociohistorical partisan attachments, may be seen as partial confirmation of Philips's speculations. Ideological elements such as racial segregation seem to set the stage for partisan affiliation rather than "critical elections," and they may require a shift in the appeal of the parties or portend a coming shift. No doubt Philips would argue that the defection of many alleged Democrats to the Nixon camp indicates that the shift has already taken place. Burnham might support the argument with historical precedent. Just as the nomination of William Jennings Bryan by the Democrats in 1896 meant the estrangement of the urban north from the Democratic party so, too, might the nomination of George McGovern in 1972 mean the estrangement of the white-ethnic and union vote from the same party.

Secondly, it is relevant to note that the group evidently most affected by this shift in the nature of the electoral tendencies is the Catholic voter. Philips argues that a two-stage process will take place among Catholic voters in the New York area. In general, they will tend to be more conservative. However, while in Baltimore and Boston this conservatism might be manifest within the ranks of the Democratic party, in New York "minority-group influences and more advanced realignment carr(y) a large number of Catholics into the ranks of the Republican electorate."[8]

At least the first part of Philips's hypothesis seems to be suggested by the present data. A greater concern for matters of racial regard seems to stand the Catholic voter apart from his non-Catholic counterparts. No doubt, Philips might argue that this finding portends the two-step process that he projects. The implication remains that the long alliance between the Catholic voter and the Democratic party--dating as it does to the periods of immigration and the formation of the great urban machines--is coming to an end as this alliance loses its usefulness. It is especially over the issue of racial concern that this break takes place.

This analysis raises two problems. The first regards the fact that it carries the findings included in the present study too far. The data outlined--and especially the causal models constructed in Chapter 6--point only to the fact that Catholic voters seem to give racial matters more weight in the determination of their vote than do non-Catholics. No shift to Republicanism is necessarily implied. In fact, large numbers of Catholics indicated their allegiance to the Democratic party. A greater concern for racial matters may mean a shift in the content of partisanship or its impact in the future (as Philips himself indicates in terms of Catholics in Boston or Baltimore) but need not mean a change in party affiliation.

A second consideration is more closely related to the nature of the impact of ethnicity in voting than to the context of partisanship. It may be that the present data say something about the Catholic voter which has little to do with shifting party loyalties. Rather, they may be one more manifestation of the fact that Catholic voters have political orientations which differ sharply from those of Jews and Protestants. The latter two groups in turn have much more similar orientations. Such were the findings

of Banfield and Wilson.[9] Their studies of bond referen-
dums in Cayuga County, Ohio, and Boston, Massachusetts,
indicated that on measures of "public-regardedness" (the
tendency to vote for the public interest and against the
ostensible social or political interest of the parochial
group) both Jews and Protestants are close to the "Yankee"
ethic of great regard for the good of the public. Catholic groups--of varying national background--generally
stand apart as more sectarian in their political orientations and voting preferences. The present data may therefore be simply another manifestation of the Banfield-
Wilson findings: Jews and Protestants tend to have similar political orientations apart from Catholics.

By and large, the data are only tentative. If nothing else, they point to the very great need for scholarly
research into the two major areas of concern here: suburban local politics and the role of ethnicity. More research must be done in the field of partisanship in the
suburbs--what is its context and content, and what relationship does it have with other variables that may precede it in the causal progression to the vote? How does
ethnicity in turn relate to partisanship? Does it play a
major role in its determination; might it play a role in
the determination of its content, social or ideological?
Finally, it is clear that more work is needed to determine the importance of the racial element in the thinking
of the suburban voter. The relationship between this element and the religious background and partisanship of the
voter seems to be crucial. What role does this factor
play in determining the content of the voter's partisanship, and how does this relate to his religious identification? The present findings suggest that the above must
form the structure of future research.

NOTES

1. See for example, R. Wood, Suburbia: Its People
and Their Politics (Boston: Houghton-Mifflin, 1952); also
B. Berger, Working-Class Suburb (Berkeley: University of
California, 1960).

2. See S. Lubell, The Future of American Politics
(New York: Harper, 1952); also J. Kramer and S. Levantman,
Children of the Gilded Ghetto (New Haven: Yale University,
1961); also S. Carlos, "Religious Participation and the
Urban-Suburban Continuum," American Journal of Sociology
(March 1970): 742-59; also S. Lieberson, "Suburbs and Eth-
nic Residential Patterns," same Journal (May 1962): 673-81.

3.   To a greater development of this point with regard to Jewish voters, please see the following: N.
Glazer, <u>American Judaism</u> (Chicago: University of Chicago,
1957); also E. Litt, "Jewish Ethno-Religious Involvement
and Political Liberalism," <u>Social Forces</u> (May 1961): 328-
32; also E. Schoenfeld, "Jewish Identity and Voting Among
Small Town Jews," <u>Sociological Quarterly</u> (Spring 1968):
170-75.

4.   For a fuller development of the role of party as
aggregator, see A. Campbell et al., <u>The American Voter</u>
(New York: J. Wiley and Sons, 1960).

5.   Wood, op. cit.

6.   W. D. Burnham, <u>Critical Elections and the Mainstream of American Politics</u> (New York: Norton, 1970);
see also, W. D. Burnham and R. Chambers, <u>The American
Party Systems</u> (New York: Oxford, 1967).

7.   K. Philips, <u>The Emerging Republican Majority</u>
(New Rochelle: Arlington, 1969).

8.   Ibid., p. 169.

9.   E. Banfield and J. Wilson, "Public-Regardedness
as a Value Premise in Voting Behavior," <u>American Political Science Review</u> (September 1964): 876-87; see also, by
the same authors, "Political Ethos Revisited," same <u>Review</u>
(December 1971): 1048-62.

BALLOT A--1972

The following is a copy of the 1972 election day ballot. Please fill it out as you did in November. If you do not recall how you voted, please fill it out as you would vote if you were voting right now.

Office	Republican Slate	Democratic Slate
President	Richard Nixon	George McGovern
Congressman	Benjamin Gilman	John Dow
State Senate	Donald Ackerson	Art Athens
State Senate	Harold Grune	John Grant
State Assembly	Eugene Levy	Joseph Thaxton
Town Justice	Andrew Codispotti	Bernard Stanger
County Sheriff	Ray Lindemann	Jack Shea
Sanitation Council	Wm. Fitzgerald	Gernard Schumann
Planning Manager	Lincoln Jones	Andrew Roselli

BALLOT B--1973

The following is a proposed ballot with candidates for local offices who may run in the coming November elections. Please fill out this ballot as you would if today were election day.

Office	Republican Slate	Democratic Slate
Supervisor	Noah Weinberg	John McAlevey
Supervisor	Alfred Murphy	John McAlevey
County Legislator	Herschel Greenbaum	Hy Jatkoff
	Alfred Murphy	Linda Winikow
	Joseph Balsamo	Sam Colman
(Choose any 6)	Lester Lepori	Lou Kurtz
	Harry Molden	Jack Shea
	Noah Weinberg	Isaac Goodfriend
	Walter Levy	Dennis Dillon
Town Board	Tom France	Bernard Charles
	Ray Kruse	Mac Wortman
	Tom Smith	Harry Siegerman
(Choose any 2)	Jack Ryan	Howard Segal
	Ray Bash	Larry Diamond
	"Red" Levy	Jack Meehan
	Sanford Dranoff	Dominick Capuano
	Leonard Jefferson	Hy Jatkoff

156

1. What is your (husband's) occupation?
2. What was the last grade you completed in school?
3. Generally speaking, in politics, with which party do you identify?
4. Would you say that you identify with the (?) party strongly, moderately, or weakly?
5. Some people feel that local affairs are important while others do not have time to study them carefully. How about you? In local elections--such as supervisor, town board, or county legislature--would you say you follow issues closely, very closely, not very closely, or hardly at all?
6. Please give your feelings about the following statements by indicating whether you agree strongly, agree, have no opinion, disagree, or disagree strongly:

    A. Local law enforcement officials have been unfairly handicapped in their attempts to prevent crime in this community;
    B. I see nothing wrong with Black people moving onto this block;
    C. Drug abuse is the major issue facing our town;
    D. Generally speaking, it makes little difference whether the Democrats or Republicans are in control in this town;
    E. I don't mind if high-rise apartment buildings are built in this area;
    F. Too much money is spent on public schools in this area;
    G. In general, there is not much difference between the candidates who run for public office in this town;
    H. People on welfare get too much for nothing;
    I. Meeting a local candidate for public office would impress me;
    J. In general, we can usually trust local officials to do what is right;
    K. I would prefer to meet such a candidate at my home, at a local shopping center, at an informal gathering, or at a political debate.

7. Do you listen to a local radio station (WRKL, WKQW)? (If so) About how often would you say you listen-- several times a week, once a week, once a month, less often? In general, which hours of the day do you listen to local radio: 8 a.m.--10 a.m., 10 a.m.--12, 12--2 p.m., 2 p.m.--4 p.m., 4 p.m.--6 p.m.?

8. When listening to news on local radio, about how much of your listening time is spent on town and county news? Would you say about 3/4, about half, about 1/4, less?

9. Many people feel that religion and ethnic background is becoming more important in American society. Is your religious preference Protestant, Catholic, Jewish, or what?

10. (If respondent is white and Catholic) (1) Generally speaking, is your national background Irish, Italian, German, Slavic, or what? (2) Would you say you identify as a (?) strongly, moderately, weakly?

11. Do you read a local newspaper? (If so) Which one? Would you say that you read it several times a week, once a week, once a month, less often?

12. Most people do not read all of a newspaper because they just don't have the time. When reading (?) which sections do you read most often?

13. In the past election, about half the people voted and half did not. This was because many were sick. How about you, did you vote?

14. Do you discuss local politics with your family, friends, or relatives? (If so) About how often do you have such discussions--would you say several times a week, once a week, once a month, less often?

Methodological Note:

Essentially, two statistical tests have been utilized in this study. The first is the chi-square test of significance: $x^2 = \frac{(e-o)^2}{0}$. This allows the analyst to determine whether the findings were statistically valid for the purposes of confirming a hypothesis, or whether they may be attributed to random distribution of the data. The minimum significance level allowed was $p = .05$ (data would have to be so validated 95 percent of the time to be considered minimally significant). For a full analysis of the use of the chi-square statistic, the interested reader is referred to H. M. Blalock's straightforward explanation in Social Statistics (New York: McGraw-Hill, 1960), especially pages 212-21.

In addition, the Pearson C contingency coefficient: $C = \frac{x^2}{\sqrt{N + x^2}}$ was used to measure the intensity of those relationships found to be significant. These tests were used to determine which variables were the most significant in relation to the dependent variables of voting behavior, attitudes, and political interest-participation.

It is recognized that certain minor difficulties result when one attempts to compare C coefficients computed from matrixes of different sizes. It has been chosen here because of its easy derivation from the chi-square formula and its simplicity. In addition, the basis of the present study does not rely purely upon the coefficient results. In any event, statistical authorities have indicated that (1) the discrepancy between the C values computed from matrixes of differing sizes is slight; (2) the formula for correcting the discrepancy is complicated and leaves room for further error; and (3) it may be impossible to correct precisely for inaccuracy, especially if the matrix is rectangular (3x4, 2x3, and so on, rather than 2x2, 3x3). The methodologist interested in these and other issues regarding the advantages and disadvantages of the use of the Pearson C contingency coefficient may consult: J. P. Guilford, Fundamental Statistics in Psychology and Education (New York: McGraw-Hill, 1965), pp. 338-39; also Q. McNemar, Psychological Statistics (New York: J. Wiley, 1969), pp. 229-30; also J. Cohen, Statistical Power Analysis for the Behavioral Sciences (New York: Academic Press, 1969), p. 216.

Banfield, E., and Wilson, J. City Politics. Cambridge: Harvard University and M.I.T., 1963.

Berelson, B.; Lazarsfeld, P.; and Gaudet, H. The People's Choice. New York: Columbia University, 1948.

_____; Lazarsfeld, P.; and Macphee, L. Voting. Chicago: University of Chicago, 1954.

Berger, B. Working-Class Suburb. Berkeley: University of California, 1960.

Blalock, H. M. Social Statistics. New York: McGraw-Hill, 1960.

Burnham, W. D. Critical Elections and the Mainstream of American Politics. New York: Norton, 1970.

_____, and Chambers, R. The American Party Systems. New York: Oxford, 1967.

Campbell, A. White Attitudes Toward Black People. Ann Arbor: University of Michigan, 1971.

_____; Converse, P.; Miller, W.; and Stokes, D. The American Voter. New York: J. Wiley, 1960.

_____. The Voter Decides. New York: Harper, 1954.

Cohen, J. Statistical Power Analysis for the Behavioral Sciences. New York: Academic Press, 1969.

Converse, P. "The Concept of a Normal Vote." In Elections and the Public Order. Edited by A. Campbell, et al. New York: J. Wiley, 1966.

Dahl, R. Pluralist Democracy in the United States. Chicago: Rand McNally, 1967.

_____. Who Governs. New Haven: Yale University, 1961.

Dobriner, W. Class in the Suburbs. Englewood Cliffs: Prentice-Hall, 1963.

_____. The Suburban Community. New York: Putnam, 1958.

Donaldson, S. The Suburban Myth. New York: Columbia University, 1969.

Douglas, H. "The Suburban Trend." In The Suburban Community. Edited by W. Dobriner. New York: Putnam, 1958.

Flanagan, W. Political Behavior of the American Electorate. Boston: Allyn & Bacon, 1968.

Fuchs, L. John F. Kennedy & American Catholicism. New York: Meredith Press, 1967.

_____. The Politics of the American Jews. Glencoe: The Free Press, 1956.

Gannon, W. Power and Discontent. Homewood: Dorsey, 1968.

Glazer, N. American Judaism. Chicago: University of Chicago, 1957.

Goldberg, A. "Discerning a Causal Pattern Among Data on Voting Behavior." In Causal Models in the Social Sciences. Edited by N. M. Blalock. Chicago: Aldine-Atherton, 1971.

Greely, A. Why Can't They Be Like Us. New York: Institute of Human Relations, 1969.

Guilford, J. Fundamental Statistics in Psychology and Education. New York: McGraw-Hill, 1965.

Harshbarger, T. Introductory Statistics. New York: Macmillan, 1971.

Key, V. O. American State Politics. New York: Knopf, 1956.

_____. The Responsible Electorate. Cambridge: Harvard University, 1966.

Kramer, J., and Levantman, S. Children of the Gilded Ghetto. New Haven: Yale University, 1961.

Lenski, G. The Religious Factor. Garden City: Doubleday, 1961.

Levey, M., and Kramer, M. The Ethnic Factor. New York: Simon & Schuster, 1972.

Lubell, S. The Future of American Politics. New York: Harper, 1952.

McNemar, Q. Psychological Statistics. New York: J. Wiley, 1969.

Merton, R. "The Latent Functions of the Machine." In Urban Government. Edited by E. Banfield. New York: The Free Press, 1969.

Miller, W., and Stokes, D. "Constituency Influence in Congress." In Elections and the Public Order. Edited by A. Campbell et al. New York: J. Wiley, 1966.

Moynihan, D., and Glazer, N. Beyond the Melting Pot. Cambridge: Harvard University and M.I.T., 1970.

Philips, K. The Emerging Republican Majority. New Rochelle: Arlington, 1969.

Reisman, D. "The Suburban Sadness." In The Suburban Community. Edited by W. Dobriner. New York: Putnam, 1958.

Simon, H. "Spurious Correlation: A Causal Interpretation." In Causal Models in the Social Sciences. Edited by N. M. Blalock. Chicago: Aldine-Atherton, 1971.

Spectorsky, A. The Exurbanites. Philadelphia: Lippincott, 1956.

Wakin, E., and Shever, J. The DeRomanization of the American Catholic Church. New York: Macmillan, 1966.

Wattel, H. "Levitown: A Suburban Community." In The Suburban Community. Edited by W. Dobriner. New York: Putnam, 1958.

Whyte, W. The Organization Man. New York: J. Wiley, 1956.

Williams, O.; Herman, H.; Liebman, C.; and Dye, T. Suburban Differences & Metropolitan Policies. Philadelphia: University of Pennsylvania, 1965.

Wirt, F.; Walter, B.; Rabinovitz, F.; and Hensler, D. On
the City's Rim. Lexington: D. C. Heath, 1972.

Wood, R. Suburbia: Its People & Their Politics. Boston:
Houghton Mifflin Co., 1959.

ARTICLES

Bachrach, P., and Baratz, M. "Two Faces of Power."
American Political Science Review (December 1962):
947-52.

Banfield, E., and Wilson, J. "Political Ethos Revisited."
American Political Science Review (December 1971):
1048-62.

_____. "Public-Regardedness as a Value Premise in Voting
Behavior." American Political Science Review (September 1964): 876-87.

Carlos, A. "Religious Participation and the Urban-
Suburban Continuum." American Journal of Sociology
(March 1970): 742-59.

Fairly, R. "Suburban Persistence." American Sociological
Review (February 1964): 38-47.

Fraser, J. "The Mistrustful-Efficacious Hypothesis and
Political Participation." Journal of Politics (May
1970): 444-49.

Hamilton, H. "The Municipal Voter: Voting and Non-
Voting in City Elections." American Political
Science Review (December 1971): 1135-41.

Hawkins, B.; Marando, U.; and Taylor, G. "Efficacy, Mistrust and Political Participation." Journal of
Politics (February 1969): 1130-36.

Janosik, G. "The New Suburbia." Current History (August
1956): 91-95.

Kramer, G. "Short-Term Fluctuations in U.S. Voting Behavior." American Political Science Review (March
1971): 131-43.

Lazerwitz, P. "Suburban Voting Trends: 1948-1956."
Social Forces (October 1960): 29-36.

Lieberson, S. "Suburbs & Ethnic Residential Patterns."
American Journal of Sociology (May 1962): 673-81.

Litt, E. "Jewish Ethno-Religious Involvement and Political Liberalism." Social Forces (May 1961): 328-32.

Lorinskas, R., and Hawkins, B. "The Persistence of Ethnic
Voting in Urban & Rural Areas." Social Science Quarterly (March 1969): 891-99.

Martin, W. "The Structure of Social Relationships Engendered by Suburban Residence." American Sociological
Review (August 1956): 446-53.

Page, B., and Brody, R. "Policy Voting & the Electoral
Process." American Political Science Review (September 1972): 979-95.

Parenti, M. "Ethnic Politics & the Persistence of Ethnic
Identification." American Political Science Review
(December 1967): 717-26.

Pomper, G. "Ethnic & Group Voting in Non-Partisan Municipal Elections." Public Opinion Quarterly (Spring
1966): 79-97.

_____. "From Confusion to Clarity: Issues & the American
Voters, 1956-1968." American Political Science Review (June 1972): 415-28.

Ranney, A., and Epstein, L. "The Two Electorates."
Journal of Politics (August 1966): 598-616.

Reisman, D. "The Suburban Dislocation." Annals of the
American Academy of Political and Social Sciences
(November 1957): 130-41.

Repass, D. "Issue Salience & Party Choice." American
Political Science Review (June 1971): 389-400.

Schoenfeld, E. "Jewish Identity and Voting Among Small-Town Jews." Sociological Quarterly (Spring 1968): 170-75.

Wirt, F. "The Political Sociology of American Suburbia: A Reinterpretation." Journal of Politics (August 1965): 647-66.

Wolfinger, R. "The Development and Persistence of Ethnic Voting." American Political Science Review (December 1965): 896-908.

_____. "Non-Decisions and the Study of Local Politics." American Political Science Review (December 1971): 1063-80.

Wood, R. "The Impotent Suburban Vote." Nation (3 March 1960): 273-74.

Zikmund, J. "Comparison of Political Attitudes & Activity Patterns in Central Cities & Suburbs." Public Opinion Quarterly (Spring 1967): 69-75.

121-22, 124; and political
interest, 77, 78, 94-95,
99, 102; and the local
media, 89; and ethnicity,
127-30, 152
Pearson C coefficient of
contingency, 26ff, 33-34,
36, 38ff, 106ff
Philips, K., 152, 155
Pomper, G., 7, 47, 74
Protestants, 7, 13, 18, 24;
and the vote, 24ff, 115ff,
142ff, 154; and political
attitudes, 53ff, 63ff; and
racial segregation, 70;
and partisanship, 72, 124;
and the local media, 81-93;
and political interest,
94ff

racial segregation, 33, 36ff,
43-46, 49, 54, 70-75, 106,
138, 150-51
Ramapo Township, 11-14, 18,
19; and the 1972 election
results, 18-19, 35, 96
Ranney, A., 105
Reisman, D., 74, 105
religion, 1, 8, 23, 24; in
Ramapo, 13-14; and the
vote, 23ff, 41-42, 43-46,
49, 70, 106ff, 120; and
political attitudes, 52ff,
63ff, 73; and racial seg-
regation, 70; and parti-
sanship, 72, 124; and po-
litical interest, 78ff,
94ff; and the local media,
81-93
Rapass, D., 74, 134
Republican Party, 18, 27;
and the suburbs, 2-3, 22,
35, 136; in Ramapo, 13;
and the vote, 33ff, 43, 49,
152; and political atti-
tudes, 64, 68; and racial
segregation, 71-72; and
religion, 72, 124; and

political interest, 92, 106

sampling procedure, 14-15,
16, 19-20, 138
Scheuer, J., 120
Schoenfeld, E., 155
Simon, H., 134
social class, 2, 3, 5, 16,
23; in Ramapo, 11-12, 19
Spectorsky, A., 74
statistical methodology, 20,
39, 43-46, 72, 106ff
suburbs, 19, 136; and the
vote, 2ff, 8, 21ff; and
political attitudes, 45ff;
and political interest,
77ff

Taylor, G., 105
transplantation theory, 2,
21, 22, 51, 52, 149
trust in government, 77, 96;
as a political attitude,
54, 61-62, 73

voting, 16, 17, 20; and the
suburbs, 2ff, 21ff, 41ff;
and ethnicity, 7-8, 43-51,
106ff, 141; in Ramapo,
18-19, 19-20; turnout, 79,
97-99

Wakin, E., 134
welfare, 54; attitudes,
67-68, 73
Whyte, W., 74, 105
Williams, O., 47, 75
Wilson, J., 2, 7, 46, 47,
75, 134, 154
Wirt, F., 3, 46, 47, 74, 75,
76
Wolfinger, R., 10, 46, 74,
134
Wood, R., 9, 47, 74, 105,
154, 155

Ziegler, H., 48
Zikmund, J., 46, 75

168

DAVID J. SCHNALL is Assistant Professor of Political Science at Staten Island Community College. He is also Adjunct Instructor of Judaic Studies at Brooklyn College and Adjunct Assistant Professor of Political Science in the Graduate Program in Public Administration at Long Island University. In addition, he serves as a consultant to the Study in Israel Program of the Tri-State Consortium for International Education at Rockland Community College.

Dr. Schnall has published widely in the areas of urban life, Middle Eastern politics, and Jewish affairs. His articles and reviews have appeared in the Annals of the American Academy of Political and Social Sciences, the Journal of Social History, the Middle East Journal, the Jewish Quarterly Review, and the Proceedings of the Association of Orthodox Jewish Scientists. He has also contributed to Judaism, Tradition, and the Jewish Spectator.

Dr. Schnall holds a B.A. and M.S. from Yeshiva University. He is an ordained rabbi and received an M.A. and Ph.D. from Fordham University.

BLACK COMMUNITY CONTROL: A Study of Transition
in a Texas Ghetto
> Joyce E. Williams

ETHNIC AND RACIAL SEGREGATION PATTERNS IN
THE NEW YORK METROPOLIS: Residential Patterns
Among White Groups, Blacks, and Puerto Ricans
> Nathan Kantrowitz

ETHNIC IDENTITY AND ASSIMILATION: THE POLISH-
AMERICAN COMMUNITY: Case Study of Metropolitan
Los Angeles
> Neil C. Sandberg
> Foreword by Herbert Gans

POLITICAL CLUBS IN NEW YORK
> Blanche Davis Blank and
> Norman M. Adler

POLITICAL SOCIALIZATION OF CHICANO CHILDREN: A
Comparative Study with Anglos in California Schools
> Chris F. Garcia

RACIAL TRANSITION IN THE INNER SUBURB:
Studies of the St. Louis Area
> Solomon Sutker and
> Sarah Smith Sutker

THE WHITE ETHNIC MOVEMENT AND ETHNIC POLITICS
> Perry L. Weed